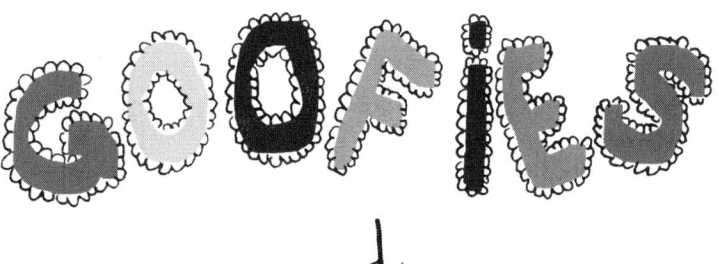

GOODIES

Have fun!
Mary D Shaw

**80+ entries from
40+ writers**

Compiled by Mary Jo Shaw

Author, *Crossroads to Convent* and *Convent to Catwalk*

Goofies and Goodies
Copyright © 2022 by Mary Jo Shaw
All rights reserved.

ISBN 978-0-578-39480-0
LCCN: 2022905072

Printed by Gorham Printing in
Centralia, WA USA

ACKNOWLEDGMENTS

What a delight to give credits and thanks to my relatives, friends and friends of friends who responded to my request for entries. It's a good thing it wasn't a contest. Too many winners!

Where do I begin?

Think about it! First, there would be no book if the **41 writers** hadn't shared their poems, true stories, etc. Their enthusiasm electrified me. I'd get comments and questions, such as, "Mary Jo, do I have some true whoppers to send you!" Or "You probably think I made up this event, but every word is for real."

Thanks to my **hubby, Chris**, for reading and correcting my typos, deleting repeated paragraphs, and inserting missing words of many stories that I wrote up from interviews, or that I had to retype into more recent Word format for the printer.

Ruth Shearer actually *volunteered* to give a final read just before sending the manuscript to Gorham Printing. What a friend and what a big help sweeping out many messy crumbs! Thank you, Ruth.

Then there is my first-cousin whom I babysat when I was about 8, **Patrick Osborn**, a retired math teacher who told his physics students: "When reading something technical, it usually doesn't start becoming clear until around third or fourth reading. Don't give up!"

While gathering stories for this GOOFIES AND GOODIES compilation, what I had dreaded finally stared me in the face. I told

Patrick that I taught myself by hit-and-miss and, when I discovered it worked, I asked myself, *"What did I just do to make an Excel spreadsheet that kept tract of authors, titles of stories, and...not only total of words for each entry...but a running total of all entries?"*

Patrick patiently and clearly proved to me what an excellent teacher he was. He walked me through the formula that had *accidently* worked. Later we numbered entries in proper sequence, and sent them from Word to Excel.

Patrick helped me merge all of the documents into one long document for the printer. He had hung in there for hours, 1200 miles away on Facetime, pitching me his teaching skills patiently and clearly, until "The End." Thanks for your loving, kind, generous tutoring, Patrick!

Thanks to my Panorama friends **Chuck and Mary Lee** (she is the award-winning author of *When Grandma's False Teeth Fly*) for asking when they could chauffeur me to Centralia to my dependable, easy-to-work-with Gorham Printing for my other books and now again for GOOFIES AND GOODIES. It's a win-win...they drive, and I treat us all to one of their favorite restaurants for lunch, desserts and extra take-home desserts.

Talk about help getting this third-round of help! **Corrine Wasmundt** laughed, "Mary Jo, I don't remember what we did three years ago when we plowed through computer screens working to get those ISBN, Library of Congress numbers, and barcodes, but we'll go at it again." And we did. You are one dependable person, Corrine. Thanks, in "triplet time."

Many thanks to **John and Melody** (our daughter) for supplying reams of printer paper. Due to Covid-19, I didn't have to load my printer with blank sides of junk mail anymore! However, I do continue to conserve with any blank sides and junk mail! Why not? To **their daughter Hope 13**, thanks for your entry and picture of your favorite pal, George. (I'm not one to touch animals, but Hope's huge Labradoodle knows that Granny Jo *loves him.* We just don't get enough hugs together!)

Way out in Texas to our son, **Chris, and wife Teresa, Sarah 17**, and **Emily 14**...kudos for your unforgettable stories, constant support and for the idea to ZOOM and enjoy dinners simultaneously. Seems we *got together* a little more often when we had to *stay at home.*

I send love to my **sisters** and families who were *almost* as excited as I was about this project.

Most importantly, I dedicate to and thank my **Father God** for sending me the lovely friends and family mentioned above, and certainly, my many (hopefully!) future readers. Also, for my health, extra time, and joy to write.

God must have a sense of humor. You'll see what I'm talking about when you experience the various talents that He has imparted to these 41 writers. I hope GOOFIES AND GOODIES gives God due praise, honor and glory in a fun, enjoyable and unique way.

WRITERS

A, Margaret
Allen, Tom
Anonymous, H.
Anonymous, S.
Ballard, Ernesta
Berner, Candace
Bowers, Bob
Chapin, Carol and Connie
Clow, Bill
Enns, Paul and MaryAnne
Fritchley, Hope
Garwood, Jean
Gernon, Dean and Rose
Geyer, Rosemary
Horton, Judy
Kay, Jerri
Lee, Mary
Lynch, Patti
Lyon, Chuck
Milne, Dave
Morrish, Kristi

Odio, Carolyn
Oldfield, Tana and Bob
Osborn, Patrick
Peterson, Evelyn
Reuter, Lucy
Rogers, Verl
Severson, Carol
Shaw, Chris Arvid
Shaw, Chris William
Shaw, Emily Anne
Shaw, Mary Jo
Shaw, Sarah Kathryn
Steckley, LeNoi
Thompson, Jeanne
Toy, Gladys
Trupp, Martha
Ulrich, Don
Vogel, Sally
Walter, Al
Williams, Lois

Fast Forwarding from the Author

The title GOOFIES AND GOODIES fast forwards *you* and wets your appetite as to what *you* might expect between the covers of this compilation of writer-entries. However, what did *I* expect or not expect?

I've heard many memoir gems for over eight decades, and I felt a two-way interest. I actually typed many of those gems into my FUNNIES FILE. Why? When I'd start sharing a *funny* with a group, I'd get to the punch line and *freeze!*

Family, friends from all over the country, and residents here in our Panorama Retirement and Convalescent Center in Lacey, WA, lit up when I hinted about gathering articles from anyone willing to share for my forthcoming book.

The first residents I spoke with burst out, "I have some really good ones...like the time...

Be careful, Reader, I see you nodding, also!

Momentum picked up when I contacted on phone, in person, emails, etc. A week later my computer tablet started receiving true stories, poems, and prose. Styles of writing and accounts offer a vast variety. *No* two entries are alike...from 14-word "one-liners" to 1400-word stories. Some articles turn on the lights *behind the scenes* of unusual careers, professions, travels, inspirations, mishaps...

You will shed tears of laughter, yet at times feel a tug on your heartstrings.

So, what did *I not* expect when mentally fast-forwarding to work on this project? **Covid-19 in 2020:** neither a goofy, nor a goodie, and it began the same month I started inviting entries for GOOFIES AND GOODIES.

However, as a positive thinker, I couldn't let my insides melt. I appreciated the *extra time* during the *stay-at-home*. I could enjoy tapping hours on my tablet with a clean conscience, and teach myself the "basics" of Excel. Columns in spreadsheet kept the writers' names alphabetically, the title of each entry, its word-count, and a running total of *all* the words.

Writers also had *extra time* for the fun of "exposing" their favorite goofies and goodies to me…to unveil and disclose to you!

So…open the book anywhere to read, but don't miss a single entry. Take it along when you'll have just a few minutes to fill.

Share the stories when the conversation turns to, "I've got a real *goodie!* I just read…"

If you enjoy it, how many others will?

Have fun!

CONTENTS

iii	Acknowledgments	16	Me? Nobody Special? *Anonymous*
vii	Writers		
viii	Fast Forwarding from the Author	17	The Voice *Lois Williams*
1	Burned Up House Guest *Al Walter*	19	A Push From Mom *Mary Lee*
5	A Wedding Oops *Kristi Morrish*	21	Two Stories. Romeo. The Cemetery *Tom Allen*
7	Widower Song *Verl Rogers*	23	Surprise Visit *Emily Shaw, age 14 in 2020*
8	Hope is Calling *Mary Jo Shaw*	26	Mildred's Lemon Pound Cake *Carolyn Odio*
9	Four Fun RVing Stories from Paul and MaryAnne Enns: *Paul and MaryAnne Enns*	28	The Best Easter Sunday Ever! *Bob Bowers*

30	Requiem *Ernesta Ballard*		52	Three Childhood Favs *Sarah Shaw*
31	Raucous Dating Game *Mary Jo Shaw*		54	Two Shorts *Verl Rogers*
34	Saints and Children Preserve Us— 5 Shorts *Lois Williams*		55	Dad Waters Garden *Understandably anonymous.*
			56	Seats I've Sat In *Evelyn Peterson*
37	Family Funnies *Shared by Tana and Bob Oldfield*		60	Depths of Denial *Anonymous #2*
40	Blood Hounds *Chuck Lyon*		61	Smellavision Memories *LeNoi Steckley*
42	A Fiery Wedding *Dean and Rose Gernon*		62	Convent to Catwalk … Writing My Story *Mary Jo Shaw*
43	What is EMHE? *Carol and Connie Chapin*		67	High Rise and Hot *Jean Garwood*
47	Virtuoso *Lois Williams*		69	Long Short Steps *Margaret A.*
48	The Heat Sheet *Don Ulrich*		70	Sedate Enjoyment *Verl Rogers*
49	Oops! *Verl Rogers*		71	The Record Quarter Mile *Tom Allen*
51	Snowed In Nome, Alaska! *Carol Severson*			

73	Two Teacher Stories *Patrick Osborn*	92	Billiard Accuracy and Excuses *Verl Rogers*
75	God Blessed America in Gentle Care *Mary Jo Shaw*	94	Depression: Home Half Block from the Alamo *Chris Arvid Shaw*
77	Easy As Pie *Verl Rogers*	97	Funds for Food and Fun *Chris Arvid Shaw*
79	Battle of the Alamo and Coronavirus *Rosemary Geyer, San Antonio, Texas*	102	The Art of Compromise *Bob Bower*
80	Whatta Wedding With Warren! *Judy Horton*	104	Gene and Me: Frankenstein *Tom Allen*
85	No "Trespassing" Fun Aging Fig Tree's Confession *Jerri Kay*	105	Finding Easter Ride *Mary Jo Shaw*
		107	A French Kiss *Sally Vogel, author of 24 books on Blurb*
86	Humorous Friend's Hope *Mary Jo Shaw*	108	Il Volo - Musicians par Excellence *Martha Trupp*
87	Death Is Close *Verl Rogers*		
89	Emily's Email *Emily Shaw, age 14*	111	Paid In Full *Lois Williams*
91	Laughs and Hugs *Hope Fritchley*	113	Beginning to Teach at 100 *Mary Jo Shaw*

114	God's Plan to Meet for Patti *Patti Lynch*	137	My Roast For My Brother's 50th Birthday Party *Sally Vogel, author, 24 books on Blurb*
116	Mad-Lib Miranda *Bill Clow*		
118	Baby Baths *Verl Rogers*	139	Electric Shock *Verl Rogers*
120	Romantic Night in Florence *Don Ulrich*	141	Warning: No Baby Bends! *May St. Peter*
		142	The Bakery *Chuck Lyon*
122	Melpomene and Me *Bill Clow*	143	Up on the House Top … …sooner or later … it just had to happen … *Dave Milne*
124	Elizabeth and Israel, 1778 *Ernesta Ballard*		
126	Gene and Me: Tricky Dick *Tom Allen*	149	Let It Go *Verl Rogers*
128	Writing Prompt Signs *Mary Lee*	151	Ernest "Ernie" Becker #1 *Jeanne D. Thompson*
130	Music Prayer's Long-Lasting Journey *Mary Jo Shaw*	153	Addition to "Ernie" Memory #2 *Jeanne D. Thompson*
134	Cotton Candy Up-tic, Miranda? *Bill Clow*	155	Christmas on the Ranch *Lucy Reuter*

157	My Romance
Verl Rogers	169	Music for the Ages
Mary Jo Shaw
159	Tantan's Teasers and Treasures
Mary Jo Shaw	172	Emily's Salad and Shoes
Emily Shaw, age 14
162	Four Favorite Shorties
Candy Berner	173	Copacabana and Extras!
Evelyn Peterson
164	Extra Day in My Life
Mary Jo Shaw	179	Chita Knew
Lucy Reuter
166	Life's Greatest Embarrassment
Candy Berner	181	Heart's Desire
Lois Williams
167	Mama and the Blue Mercury
Lucy Reuter	185	Did You Enjoy Goofies And Goodies?

Burned Up House Guest

Al Walter

We missed the first clue that things were not as they seemed—teeth marks shaping a third-floor window sill. The man trying to sell us the house attributed the teeth carving to a high-strung dog penned in the room by a previous owner. The confined pet, he explained, tended to chew on things during thunder-and-lightning storms.

Outside the house, among several old maple and elm trees, thrived a large conclave of very active squirrels. They darted, climbed, fled, jumped, flew, chased, swung, fell, fought and trapezed as though possessed or fortified with steroids. The unusual colony seemed very happy and noisy, screeching endlessly.

To us, it was a rare scene. In a scary way, it was refreshing to witness such merriment among these vibrant animals and potentially new neighbors. However, we should have worried about their sustained, high level of frenzy. Probably another reason why we should not be surprised by coming events.

My wife, Kitty, and I liked the old three-story, stucco-on-stone house built in 1914. It came with 14 rooms and 54 windows. Daughters Carol, Eileen and Mary Beth had already identified cool places to play and raise a new puppy. So we bought it, with its ancient wood-shingled roof and soon-to-explode furnace. We got the extrovert squirrels free.

A few days after the sale, we had our first encounter with a squirrel neighbor. In a second-floor bedroom, daughter Eileen was peering through a window, watching a squirrel strutting out a tree limb toward her. She felt secure behind the glass and a sturdy screen. Besides, the tip of the branch was a good 15 feet from the window.

Without hesitation, the new neighbor leaped/flew the gap between the branch tip and window and hit the screen with a heavy clunk, curling its claws around the screen mesh to hang on. Eileen screamed with alarm at the unexpected landing and, instinctively, rapped on the window to encourage the squirrel to let go.

Instead, the squirrel bared its teeth and snarled in defiance. That's not what your ordinary peanut-eating squirrel does in the municipal park.

Eileen, then treated us to a scream that was easily a No. 10 on the scream scale, and fled the room. The squirrel almost seemed to resent our being there. Could it have been an inhabitant before we came? Another clue that these creatures may enter our lives in some unforeseen way.

About a week later, as the weather cooled, I gazed with both admiration and concern at a group of squirrels swarming over our roof like a SWAT team on a dangerous assignment. A man who introduced himself as a roofer positioned himself next to me.

"You know, you got a big bunch of squirrels that would like to get into your house." I agreed it did seem that way.

"What you ought to do is cover that chimney top with hardware cloth to keep them out before they become a problem," he intoned. "That's how they get in, you know."

He told me that he had advised the previous owner to take similar action, after checking out the chimney top for them, but they rejected his offer to do it. I told him to proceed with the operation.

Afterward, with the squirrels ostensibly sealed out of the house, the time came to build a nice fire in the fireplace. The family crowded around the fireplace and cheered the warmth provided by the licking flames.

Soon a heavy clump of something looking like a big nest dropped down the chimney, falling with a heavy splat on the fiery hearth. We had no idea there was a nest in the chimney, but we felt secure, knowing it was confined in the hearth behind the steel chain hearth safety guard.

That mood changed abruptly when something still alive and burning hopped out of the fireplace, punching through the chain like it was a wet paper.

Now we had a flaming squirrel running at top speed through all parts of the living room like a run-away blow torch, pausing under drapes and upholstered furniture in frantic pain, threatening to send the entire house into flames.

We also had a fast, shrieking exodus of family members who dashed into the kitchen. Once there, they climbed onto the kitchen table and howled in protest to the unexpected event. They didn't want a fiery squirrel gyrating at their feet.

What to do quickly to save the house and put the squirrel out of its misery?

Water wasn't the answer because the squirrel moved too fast. Being new residents, I had left the fire extinguisher at the hardware store for recharging.

Top priority—the squirrel had to go.

I stopped Carol, our oldest daughter, before she could flee with the other escapees. She was terrified, but agreed to quickly grab the metal waste basket from the kitchen, give it to me and stand by.

From the time the squirrel started his flaming circles, I tracked its movement, yelling and clapping hands, not allowing him to stop near anything flammable. He got good traction on our area hooked rug, but literally spun his wheels like an automobile tire on slick ice when he hit the hardwood floors beyond the rug. I blessed Kitty and her penchant for maintaining highly waxed floors.

Carol quickly caught onto the squirrel's skidding problem. She understood when I asked her to clap and yell and chase the squirrel around the far end of the room, then down the side toward the front door.

When she prodded the squirrel into high gear, I yelled from the opposite end of the floor, sending the squirrel into skid mode. With the poor critter sliding, it skid into my waiting metal waste basket. When I felt it hit bottom, I swung open the door with one hand and hurled the squirrel out of the basket with the other hand.

It flew through the air, smoking and dropped to the ground. The poor animal rolled on the grass and ran out of sight. We found the charred carcass of a burned squirrel about a week later in shrubbery near the house.

We had more ventures with the squirrels after that, but none so painful.

A Wedding Oops

Kristi Morrish

It was a scrumptious sunny day for a lawn wedding at Pt. Defiance Park in Tacoma, WA. My sophisticated New York work friend, Paula, invited her friends and family, mainly from the East coast, to her garden wedding. Eager to meet them, I set out early for the afternoon event.

I was unfamiliar with the park roads winding through lush garden settings, small gazebos, and pagodas. I came upon a lovely lawn wedding set-up and was delighted to find ample parking nearby. White everywhere is so inviting in a garden. Flowers. Seating. Tents. Tables. Candles. And the center aisle awaiting the bride's footsteps. Anticipation builds as I take a seat near the front aisle along with others. Not recognizing guests near me, I introduced myself as a friend of the bride.

No time to visit, the ceremony was beginning. As each attendant passed, I was struck by how different each one seemed from Paula's descriptions of her bridal party. How great is diversity, I thought. Just like at every wedding, I grew excited to see the bride. As the wedding march filled the air, I turned to watch my friend whisper-step down her white aisle.

I was surprised to see someone I thought was another attendant, pushing an older gentleman in a wheelchair down the aisle. I suddenly realized this IS the bride pushing her ESCORTING FATHER down the aisle, both with tears of happiness and expectancy. The bride was not Paula. But I was so caught up in the beauty and emotion of their moment—I cried. No wonder no one looked familiar, I WAS AT THE WRONG WEDDING! Yet so touched by their shared moments, I just melted into their joy.

Before my presence was discovered by strangers, I quickly darted away to search for Paula's wedding. I made it in time for the reception and extended my apologies. Paula was highly amused! I'm still laughing.

Widower Song

Verl Rogers

After she died, I kissed her cooling cheek.
The body a husk, her soul was gone.
We had 58 years together,
Good memories remain.
We grew old together.
Golden years then, golden now,
Family, friends and laughter,
But she's not here.

———

Illness, pain, bandages, wounds, pills all gone.
She now lives with God, no need for
Breath, heartbeat, motion or body.
No husband, wife nor children.
No violence, anger, hatred,
Yet heaven is full of love, family, friends
Who went before.
I thank God for her life, then and now…
But I still cry.

Verl Rogers. March 6, 2019. Permission to print

Hope is Calling

Mary Jo Shaw

When our granddaughter Hope was about three years old, often we were blessed after retiring to have her over to play and baby sit. Our daughter Melody and hubby John lived within walking distance from our home.

Hope would grab her little chair, park it at the long alphabet chart under the kitchen bar pronouncing and fingering the letters. I also was teaching her counting and reading numbers. But I especially remember showing her how to read my phone number and to memorize the numerals...good for her little brain cells. Right? She learned to dial and to call me. We had been hearing that when there was an accident or someone was in trouble, cell phones could be a life saver. Melody and John were among the first in the family to own a cell phone. You have to remember that in those early days of cell phones, you paid by the minute or paid less by selecting preplanned blocks of usage, etc. There was no such thing as *unlimited* calls.

A few days later my landline phone rang. Hope and I enjoyed talking about her little dolls and stuffed animals, and when she might be coming over to spend the day again. My heart thrilled to be bonding over the phone with my little granddaughter.

After a nice long stretch of time, I asked, "Hope, I'm so glad you called me. Can Granny talk to Mommie or Daddy now?"

She quickly whispered, "No...No, Granny, you can't talk to her now. Mommie doesn't know I'm in my closet using her cell phone."

Hope doesn't recall the incident, but those memories still whisper deep in the cells of my own quickening heart.

Four Fun RVing Stories from Paul and MaryAnne Enns:

#1. Watching How Tall Your RV is, is Important!

Paul and MaryAnne Enns

Back in the 1990s we bought our first fifth-wheel trailer together with my parents from an RV dealer in Portland. The fifth-wheel initially went to my folks' place in Toutle, WA. Dad thought they'd be able to take some trips with it. Mary Anne and I were living in Southern California.

Not long after we bought that fifth-wheel, we flew into Portland and went up to Toutle. My folks' place was directly across from the school in Toutle—on the highway up to Mt. St. Helens.

The next morning, I hooked dad's Dodge Ram pick-up to the fifth-wheel. I was a bit nervous of what driving a pick-up truck pulling a 25-foot fifth-wheel trailer would be like. But I figured my experience of driving hay-trucks in my youth—to say nothing of plenty of school and church bus driving over the years—that I would be OK. And by and large, it has been.

Leaving my folks' place, we went about a quarter mile to Gilmore's Shell gas station and mini-mart to fill-up the truck.

I carefully drove the truck and trailer between the store and the row of gas pumps and filled 'er up. Feeling pretty good that I'd avoided hitting the over-hang of the building, we began pulling-out. We heard a crashing sound! Not good!

I jammed on the brakes, got out, and saw that the front corner of the fifth-wheel had hit the rain-down spout. It was one of those kinds of down-spouts that comes out of the gutter before turning toward the building. And it was on an outside corner of the store.

The good news was there was no damage to the fifth-wheel. The bad news was I'd knocked loose the gas station's down-spout and torn the rain-gutter!

Inside the store, I asked for the manager. I explained what had happened. Together we went out and looked at the damage. He said that he'd get it repaired and send me the bill.

A little bit of background information. I grew up in Toutle and knew the original store owner and his kids. The guy I was talking to, Greg, had been in school when I graduated from high school. My dad retired from teaching at Toutle Lake HS and remained active in the community.

Back to the store manager. I knew who he was, but Greg didn't recognize me. After all, it'd been about thirty years earlier that I'd graduated from HS and moved away. He asked me for my name and address. I said, "Paul Enns and I live down in Southern California."

With that the store manager, who actually was the *owner*, exclaimed, "Why Paul, I didn't recognize you. I haven't seen you for years. I'd heard that you were down in California someplace. How are you doing?"

Before leaving I gave him my name, address, and phone number and asked that he send the bill. He said he would.

That bill never arrived because it was never sent. Several months later, when we were back in Toutle, I went into the mini-mart and asked Greg for the bill. He said that just wasn't something he could send, given the esteemed role my dad had in the community.

#2. When Jill Was Right, But...

Having a GPS in the RV has been helpful. Early on we *named the voice* in our GPS—"Jill." Several years ago, a group of us from Panorama Retirement's "After Eight Group" set-up a camping trip to the Offutt Lake Resort Campground. This was shortly after Mary Anne and I moved into Panorama and not long after the After Eight group was formed. I was still learning how to get around this area. I entered Offutt Lake Resort as our destination and began following GPS Jill's directions.

We went *south* on College, crossed Yelm Highway, and were soon on Rainier Road. Jill told us to turn right on Stedman Road, and then right on Waldrick Road. A couple of miles later we obeyed and took a left on Old Highway 99. Our Garmin (formally ProNav) showed that it was only about a mile until we were to turn left on Offutt Lake Road.

But then a roadside sign told us that we were approaching a *railroad overcrossing* that was 12'6" above the roadway. I slowed, then stopped the 36' long Winnebago motorhome just before going under the tracks. A sign above the roadway *enforced* the fact that the bottom of the overcrossing was 12'6".

The problem before and above us was that our motorhome was 12'7" at its highest point! What to do? Since there wasn't any traffic behind us, I quickly got out, climbed up the rear ladder and eye-balled whether or not the top of the RVs satellite TV dome would clear the bottom of the overcrossing! I thought there was space, went back into the motorhome and shared that belief with Mary Anne.

She wisely had already decided that wasn't going to happen! She got out, walked alongside the roadway a couple of hundred feet to a spot where she could warn south-bound traffic that there was a motor-home backing up to an area where the shoulder was wider.

That's where I executed a nifty three-point turn-around on the highway.

We headed back *north* to Waldrick Road so we could go around the east end of Offutt Lake and get to the campground. We wondered why we hadn't seen any warning signs after we'd turned onto Old 99. Approaching Waldrick, we saw a sign just *south of that intersection.* We'd missed seeing it earlier!

A GPS unit is helpful. But don't believe everything you hear!

#3. Watch How the Rear-End Swings

A week after hitting the rain gutter at the Shell gas station in Toutle, we were near Cottage Grove, Oregon, visiting one of Mary Anne's brothers and his *wife. They live on a one-lane street that has white wooden fences on each side of* the lane. It was our first time in the pasture alongside their house. Getting in and out of the pasture was through a steel field-fence. The gate opening was about 12'. The fifth-wheel was 8' wide. Theoretically, there was 2' clearance on either side.

But because the lane was so narrow, I couldn't go straight in through the gate. I had to do it at an angle. Getting in was OK. Getting out wasn't!

After I got the truck and the front of the fifth-wheel through the gate, I had to make a hard-right turn. No problem, except that the rear driver's side of the fifth-wheel swung out further than I'd planned! There was an ugly encounter with the steel gate, leaving a 1' x 3' gash in the aluminum siding! **Ouch!**

It was a lesson that cost afterwards. But never, ever, knock on wood, has anything like that happened again!

#4. Better Get That Truck Out of There—Tide's Comin' In!

Several days after I'd caused injury to the back-end of the fifth-wheel, we were camping in Fort Stevens State Park, near Astoria. It's a lovely campground with the ocean on the west and the Columbia River to the north.

Our final morning there, we took dad's pick-up truck north of the campground onto Clatsop Spit. We stopped and walked up the jetty observation tower. Our second stop was at the end of the paved road at a wildlife viewing area. Our third stop should never have happened!

Leaving the wildlife area, I spotted a paved roadway that headed out to the Columbia River. When the pavement stopped, Mary Anne strongly suggested that we turn around. I mentioned that there were tire tracks ahead of us. We could see the river about a hundred feet ahead. I could also see several pick-up trucks out there. People were fishing. And Cape Disappointment was over on the Washington side!

So, I drove into the sand near the river's edge…and got very stuck in the two-wheel drive pick-up truck! Not to worry. "I'll dig us out!" But my dad didn't have a shovel in the truck's tool bin.

There were plenty of driftwood boards all around us. Using a small plank, I dug trenches, laid-down boards in front of the tires and got the truck moving—briefly. But the passenger side of the truck was lower than the driver's side. And the boards were wet, causing the back-end of the truck to slide *off* my little "roadway."

After two or three attempts to get the truck out of the sand, and causing it to dig in deeper each time, I got on the cellphone and called an auto club towing. They came out from Astoria. It took 30-45 minutes for them to arrive.

All that time, the tide was coming in! The Columbia River was getting nearer and nearer the truck!

When the tow-truck driver finally called, he said they couldn't come out onto the beach! But they had an all-wheel tow-truck back in Astoria. He told us it'd be another 30-45 minutes before he'd be back.

In the meantime, the tide kept rising! A couple of guys were fishing in their boat. They came over, and from about 25' off-shore one of them said, "You need to get that truck out of there because the tide is coming in!" We let the helpful fishermen know that a tow-truck was on its way. Their parting words were, "Good luck. Hope they get you out before the river gets you!"

When I first got stuck, the shore-line was about 25 feet away. By this time the tires on the passenger side of the truck were in the water!

Finally, the tow-truck arrived. It was an all-wheel drive WWII jeep-type rig. They drove onto the beach, backed-up and hooked us up. The driver put it in gear, and promptly got stuck in the sand—all six wheels! By this time, the Columbia River was up above the passenger-side step! It was nearly at the bottom of the door!

The tow-truck driver's helper hopped-out and unhooked us. With all six wheels engaged, the tow-truck easily got unstuck and drove about fifty-feet ahead of us onto solid ground.

The helper then began running the cable from the winch back to us. That winch was so slow. It seemed like it took another ten minutes to get the cable to the pick-up and hook us up. By that time, if Mary Anne had opened the passenger door, the Columbia River would have begun coming into the cab!

The helper hustled back to the tow-truck and started winching us in! Even though it seemed that we were only being winched by the inch, it worked. We were pulled out and able to drive onto solid ground!

All the time we were waiting for the second tow-truck, I was thinking, "Here we are on our first trip with dad's fairly new pick-up truck. I sure hope we can get it unstuck before the River gets us!"

By the time we were unstuck, I'd figured out that the pick-up trucks that we could see along the river were all four-wheel drive! I'd pretty well figured out to not take a two-wheel drive onto soft sand like that.......well—almost figured that out!

Update: These events happened over a two-week period in 1994. Since then, we've had three subsequent RVs. We've driven them over 100,000 miles and stayed in approximately 300 places. Other than a couple of minor scratches from bushes, there have been no more self-inflicted accidents or damage to our RVs!

Me? Nobody Special?

Anonymous

I was such a professional business-office secretary, I was issued an electric typewriter. Handling clients doing business over the phone, I felt comfortable and enjoyed my job. Soon we knew each other's names by their voices.

At times, a regular would need to come into the office to sign prepared papers that waited in a smart open box at the corner of my desk.

On one such occasion, a client opened the door, and immediately with side-glance, blurted, **"Oh, you're not so special!"**

Today I, Mary Jo Shaw, asked my friend to share a story for this book…long or short. Instantly, she smiled and shared the *above* incident saying, "I wasn't angry or even upset, just curious about what he meant with those words. I'm not bothered either. Funny, I just keep recalling that story."

She and I chuckled together about it.

I came home, and I'm typing on (and sometimes speaking into) my 2019 Microsoft Surface Pro. And I'm thinking. My friend is kind, thoughtful, giving, and inspiring in many ways. She shares her love of God, and I know He loves her. She's not special…she's *very* special and in a special way…a way that counts!

The Voice

Lois Williams

*"...and behold the LORD passed by, and a great and strong
wind rent the mountains, and brake in pieces the rocks
before the LORD; but the LORD was not in the wind; and
after the wind and an earthquake, but the LORD was not in the
earthquake; and after the earthquake a fire; but the LORD
was not in the fire; and after the fire a still small voice."*
1 Kings 19:11-12

*Feeling bereft sometimes
when I have done all the things
I supposed I must do to please God,
and He seems so far away,
I stand complaining,
"Where are You, God?*

*Your still, small voice,
a gentle whisper...
do I seek it in a whirlwind,
a flurry of activity?*

*Your still, small voice,
a gentle whisper...
is it audible in the earth-quaking changes
I try to make in my world?*

Your still, small voice,
a gentle whisper...
is it audible in the earth-quaking changes
I try to make in my world?

Your still small voice
a gentle whisper...
can I hear it in the fire
of my zeal to do His work?

Your still, small voice,
a gentle whisper...
is it drowned out by
the clamor of flapping wings
as I try to fly alone?

Do I need a hearing aid?

Reprinted by permission, from "Psalms From The Pathway",
Xulon Press © 2003 by Lois Williams
Email: <u>fredlowill@msn.com</u>

A Push From Mom

Mary Lee

In 1971, I attended Central Piedmont Community College in Charlotte, North Carolina. Mama drove me to class. I was 19 years old, but had zero interest in getting my driver's license because I was directionally impaired and terrified of being lost. An impossible combination when it comes to driving.

Every morning, we drove past a military service-recruiting center. There were large posters on the sidewalk, out in front of the building, that advertised a great life in the Army, Air Force, Navy and Marines. Mama often mentioned the posters as we rode by. I paid no attention to them.

After my first class, I had an hour break before my next class, so Mama picked me up and we went to a Greek restaurant about a block from the college. We had Cokes and éclairs ... our absolute favorite snack. Five days a week, Mama encouraged me to serve in the military each time we drove by the recruitment office.

Early on, I was positive I could never be in the military. I was five feet and five inches tall and weighed only 97 pounds. I was sure they would not want such a scrawny person. Even if they did, I was positive I could not leave home and my family. Mama was a persistent woman. What's more, she knew it was my only way "out of the nest" to pursue a career. She made her mind up to make it happen. I didn't stand a chance.

Mama convinced me that I should look into the possibility of military service. Weeks before graduation, I went to the recruiting center.

At 19, I only looked 15 so when I talked with the Army Recruiter, he wrongly assumed that I was a high school student. He told me, "Go home eat some bananas, put some meat on your bones, and come back in a couple of years."

Furious, I stomped down the hall to the Navy Recruiter's office, plopped in a chair, stared at the recruiter, and asked the "all time" stupid question, "Do you have to know how to swim to join the Navy?"

Patiently, he said, "Yes, but we will teach you."

I replied, "No Thank You!" while backing out his office door.

Knowing I couldn't possibly be a Marine, I decided this isn't going to work. I scurried through the hallways like a rat in a maze trying to get out of the building.

Crying so hard, I nearly collided with a fatherly looking man in an Air Force uniform.

He was drinking a cup of coffee and eating a donut. Between bites, he asked, "What's wrong little girl?"

I cried out in frustration. "I'm not a little girl! I am 19 years old, soon to be a college graduate. I tried to join the Army, but I am not old enough or fat enough. I tried to join the Navy, but I'm too afraid to learn to swim. I'm not tough enough to be a Marine. So, what is left?"

Laughing, compassionately, he said, "Come with me. I think the Air Force is where you will be best appreciated.

Mary Lee is the author of 5 Children's Books including When Grandma's False Teeth Fly.

Two Stories. Romeo. The Cemetery

Tom Allen

Romeo

Gene and I usually spent our high school lunch time in a cemetery. It was only three blocks from school past a flower shop. In the shop stood a nickel, candy-bar machine. It generously provided fine desserts at lunch...really *very* generously! After putting in our coin, continuous pulling on the handle would result in a continuous supply of loot. All those bars were good except the Romeo bar. It had rounded ends and was chocolate covered. Inside, it was filled with a mixture of raisins, nuts and other items. It tasted terrible and looked like something a dog had deposited on the sidewalk! One bite was enough to discourage the eater.

 I found a Romeo bar again while visiting my grandparents. I bought it and said we would give a playmate five cents if he could eat it. The challenge was accepted, and he ate it all. Then we informed him that it really was chocolate-coated dog poop! He ran into his house, and we went home to Grandma. Later that day, Grandma said she just received a phone call from her neighbor's mother complaining about the joke we played on her son. She had taken him downtown to have his stomach pumped to remove the dog poop. Grandma even smiled when we explained that it was only a Romeo candy bar!

The Cemetery

Oh, the cemetery! It was peaceful and interesting here, especially the little brick house. The panel above the door was broken out and revealed three coffins inside. We noticed that many people would look into the house. We also noticed a hole in the rear that penetrated the wall. A piece of hose would fit into that hole. When I moaned into the hose, it was amplified inside, as if coming from the coffins! Gene would signal me when someone was looking into the broken door panel, and I would give my best moan.

No peeper stayed in place, but quickly ran away in terror!

Surprise Visit

Emily Shaw, age 14 in 2020

Here's Emily's side of her story:

Oohh! I have a really good one!

Remember that time I went to Washington all by myself? You and Pawpaw came over to Aunt Melody and Uncle John's house, and they'd told you that you'd meet a friend of Hope's. Her name was Emily (and Hope DID actually have a friend named Emily). Y'all came over and when Hope and I came downstairs, you and Pawpaw stared at me for a moment, then said I looked exactly like your granddaughter. Then you realized it actually was me. We had a good laugh after that!

Here's her Granny Jo's recall (that's me, author of this book):

Chris and I retired at Panorama for seniors. We did not know it, but in the summer of 2019, our granddaughter Emily Shaw packed her flight bag in Leander (north of Austin, TX) for her first trip alone. She was to visit us in Lacey, WA, her Aunt Melody (our daughter), Uncle John, and her cousin Hope, 12 years old.

I was told that while planning the trip, Emily had said, "Mom, I'm so excited! Every time I talk with Granny Jo, I'm afraid I'm going to give the secret away. She and Pawpaw are going to be soo surprised. Aunt Melody says unless it's really important, she's not calling Granny and Pawpaw for fear she will spill the beans."

The next day here in Washington, Melody phoned me (Granny). "Mom, would you and Dad like to come over tonight for supper? Hope is having her friend over. We thought we'd pick up Hope's and Emily's favorite pizza. We'll also pick up some fried chicken and sides." Melody *froze*, but tried to cover up and distract that she'd mentioned *Emily!* She continued talking like a recorder on **fast speed**: "Yeah, and maybe we'll play games outside, maybe John will decide to BBQ the chicken. Oh, I dunno. Needta straightn' up the house some andthe downstairs powderroom.How'er you n Dad doin'?Ohdear, I gotta go."

I sensed that Melody suddenly seemed a bit stressed. "Oh!....Yes, we'd love to go to your house. If you pick us up a little earlier, I can help you pick up the house. I can do the powder room and..."

"OHH.NO.Mom,that's.okay.gotta go."

"Well, eh...what time are you picking us up?

"Ohyeah," Melody blurted. "About.three.gottago.BYE!"

BUZZ...BUZZ...BUZZ...

I shook my head while looking into the phone receiver, and placed it onto the phone-cradle. "Chris, we're going to Melody's for supper tonight. Hope's friend Emily is going to be there, too. I offered to help them, if they picked us up earlier, but don't think she needed me to help. Anyway, they're picking us up at three."

Chris opened the pantry. "I'll take a couple of bags of pecans and cashews. They like those. I'll put them by the door."

A few hours later, John turned into their driveway with Chris and me. The garage door yawned wide open. Hope didn't greet us at the door to the house as she usually did. I figured she was probably helping her mom, Melody.

John led us into the house just in time for Hope and her friend to greet us at the bottom of the staircase. Everyone crowded in the small area leading to the nearby kitchen.

Before anyone had a chance for introductions, I had ended up standing *right next* to the friend and offered, "Oh, hi! I'm Hope's Granny Jo." I stopped... stepped back from the young girl to take a studied, better look at her face. "Haven't I met you before? You look so familiar."

Stunned, with bulging eyes, Pawpaw Chris burst out, "You look **exactly** like our granddaughter, Emily!!"

Emily grinned such a huge smile, everyone burst out laughing.

At the suddenly loud, shocking commotion Chris and I shouted out, alternating, You ARE Emily!!! When did you get here? You came all by yourself? How long have you been here..."

Above the resounding joyful noise, I begged for tissues to mop my tears of joy and pointed, "Look at Pawpaw. He's so excited, he's red in the face."

Melody recounted inviting us over the phone to come to supper: "I wondered if you had caught on."

I exclaimed, "I remember that phone call. You *did* say that Hope's friend was Emily, but we just figured the friend's name was Emily, too." Whooping hilarity again. "I never ever put two and two together that she was OUR Emily. What a fantastic surprise!"

As the evening progressed, Emily kept getting hugs from all of us. We called our son Christopher, and Teresa (Emily's parents in Leander, TX), so they could get in on the enthusiastic racket. We revealed our thoughts, emotions and feelings step by step from the initial phone-call-invitation, to the moment of hanging up the phone, to driving up to the house.

Moments never to forget and always to remember...thanks to Melody, John, Hope, son Christopher, Teresa, Sarah (who was at camp and didn't get to come) and to Emily! We are blessed!

Mildred's Lemon Pound Cake

Carolyn Odio

1 lb of butter
2 cups sugar
6 eggs (the egg whites are folded in at very last)
2 cups of flour
2 oz of lemon extract

In the flour & sugar mixture, mix the butter in.
Mix in the egg yolks and lemon extract and add to flour mixture.
Fold in the beaten egg whites.
Bake at 300 degrees for 1 ½ hrs.
Makes 4 little loafs or 2 bread loafs.

Extra (optional) only if want to make a "fruit cake" add these:

1 lb white raisins dredged in ¼ cup flour
½ lb candied cherries
2 cups coarsely chopped pecans

(I tweaked it by removing the fruit cake ingredients, as Mildred had always included those ingredients.)

Family story:

This recipe comes from Mildred (Pearson) Porritt of Lincoln, NE—my mother's sister. She would send these loaves out to the relatives every Christmas. We waited eagerly for Mildred's Lemon Cake.

When I was learning to bake, the recipe was written on an old tattered 3x5 card. The lemon extract was written as "2-1 oz lemon extract. The dash had worn away and I read it as 2 1 oz lemon extract. I was looking for 21 (1 oz) bottles of lemon extract. I marched off to the grocery store and cleared out their shelves of lemon extract. I even summoned the manager to ask if he had any more lemon extract—he didn't. (You should have witnessed the confusion on his face.) Of course, eventually I realized the mistake. I believe it took me 10 years to use up my supply of lemon extract!

The Best Easter Sunday Ever!

Bob Bowers

Easter has always been a favorite day of mine—even better than Christmas Day. I was born March 22nd and that was usually the beginning of Spring or close to it. Flowers were beginning to blossom, and trees leaf out. In the church Lent was waning and Easter Sunday was just around the corner.

In the mid-30's and 40's when I was a child the church was the place to be on Easter Sunday. Women and girls dressed in brilliant white accented by lovely pastels. Color was everywhere. Bouquets of flowers filled the chancel. My mother, the organist and choir director of our little church, chose lively Easter music for the organ and choir. After church we gathered at my mother's parents' home for a sumptuous Easter dinner, over which Grandpa gave thanks to God. We cousins, freed from our Easter duds, had a great time playing on the greening grass of the front yard.

Easter changed some over the years, but it never lost first place in my list of holidays. It matured with my own maturity and changing life, but it was still Easter. This year I feared the Easter Holiday might be ruined. The corona virus was rising to its full stature in our society. Quarantines, hospitalizations, distancing, cancelling gatherings of humans, and shutting down churches were items sure to ruin our Easter. Our church had been closed at least two or three weeks before Easter Sunday. We scrambled to provide an Easter service that would unite us in celebration. "That will never happen," I whispered quietly to myself.

With the aid of modern social networking, we had our Easter Service. It was the best Easter Sunday ever! Somehow the presence of our leaders, the playing and singing of our musicians, the familiar hymns and worship songs, and the mood of celebration and thankfulness they conveyed made the day special—more special than usual. I was in my own apartment—simply me. But the congregation and our preachers were there to help me feel connected to each of them and loved by God. And, I live in a retirement complex that is dedicated to preserving my health and safety. What more could anyone ask, for the best Easter celebration ever! Amen!

Requiem

Ernesta Ballard

I am sitting on the sand. My shoes and socks are scattered with my pack and umbrella. Just 100 feet away waves roll in from the ocean. Just behind me is a rocky cliff that shades the Iberian sun. Soon I will open my umbrella and lie under its protection to sleep. The last steps of my journey lie ahead on this shore. I will release my husband's ashes along with burned notes from my children. This was my goal. With his scattered remains I will leave as much sorrow as I can.

I have followed a path worn by thousands in their own pilgrimage. I have walked most of the way alone with my memories and dreams. Farms, fields and villages blur. My beach is deserted. I am ready.

Five hundred miles of meditation have prepared me.

Raucous Dating Game

Mary Jo Shaw

I had been in a convent for 13 years, but left in January to recoup from extreme overwork. It was still early summer, but even spring can be humid and hot in San Antonio. My sister Patti and I stopped at the food court in North Star Mall after selecting economical, cooler clothes for me.

"Mary Jo, when Dr. Bailey asked you to take a leave of absence, he wanted you to relax, live, and date—like a normal single woman."

"Yes, but I don't know anyone."

"I understand. It's tricky. These first months have been hectic, and it's been new for you."

"So how do I meet reputable men in their 30s, willing to go out occasionally and only until next January—with an undercover nun?"

"Joe and I have known Ivan for years. He's a confirmed bachelor, Catholic, and has many other good friends. We're invited to Paul and Carol's condo to swim on Saturday. Ivan's invited. They're all eager to meet you."

"That sounds like a good idea," I said, although a little apprehensive. I hadn't dated since I was sixteen.

Saturday: Patti, Joe and I arrived in our swimsuits under our loose beach tops. Patti introduced me to Paul and Carol; then Ivan bounced through the pool gate right after us. He was physically fit, curly haired, blond, jovial and personable. Tall, hand-planted palm trees hovered over us to shade the pool.

The six of us had the area to ourselves. Joe, Paul and Ivan constantly teased, even elbowed each other into the pool. "Hey, buddy, watch out! I'll get you back after that one!" On and on—shooting water or water-soaked foam balls at each other.

We enjoyed playing Marco Polo as if we were kids, or aiming a foam ball into a floating water tube.

Carol served simple cold drinks and the three guys had a beer each. Soon we were into fun that was more rambunctious: splashing each other, popping water from clammed palms and trying to outdo each other with the creativity of getting each other wet amid the amusement and active arm swinging.

Disaster approached.

Ivan went under water and motioned me to climb onto his shoulders so I'd be higher than the others were. I did. He held my legs over his chest until only my feet were dragging in the water.

It was a balancing act: I had nothing to hold onto except Ivan's head, hair and ears. I tried to avoid mutilating him.

Disaster happened!

I swooped up a tsunami amid yells of hilarity as I flanged into the deep water behind Ivan. He turned around as I popped up for air. My eyes—even with the edge of the water—did not want to believe what I saw.

Everyone howled as I stared at two, foam, swimsuit falsies bobbing back and forth on waves between Ivan's bulging eyes and mine! I fought to grab them, but not being a swimmer, I was hanging on to Ivan with one hand. With the other I jabbed erratically as falsies floated in opposite directions. Eventually, the little monsters zigzagged the white capped waters to where I could touch bottom on my two big toes.

I water-danced a frenzied tarantella to the accompaniment of loud cries of laughter.

What was I to do, except to snatch the defiant little items, drown myself in humility under water for replacement, come up for air again and join the amusement? I needed a wake-up call from that dream, but even our deafening ricochet of hilarity didn't end my nightmare. That's how I met Ivan.

Mary Jo Shaw
Reprinted from my memoir Convent to Catwalk 2017
Maryjoshaw3@gmail.com

Saints and Children Preserve Us—
5 Shorts

Lois Williams

Author of four books, poet, speaker

Falling Apart

I was in the swimming pool with my granddaughter, who was about 10 at the time. We had had a wonderful day, playing on the swings at the neighborhood park and just enjoying each other. I wasn't used to so much exercise…So throughout the day I had hurt my shoulder and stubbed my toe, twisting my back as well. As we were splashing each other, I noticed she was getting ready to treat me to a major splash, so I turned quickly to avoid it, and I felt something give in my knee. At my yelp of pain, she asked, "Oh, Grandma, did you hurt yourself… again?" I answered, "Yes, Honey, but don't worry. When you get old, everything falls apart at once." To which, very concerned, she quavered, "Oh, I hope it's not TODAY!"

Flavors

A very picky eater, our grandson Joel, was hard to please. We were babysitting one particular time, and discovered that he really was fond of the dinosaur-shaped chicken nuggets. It was all he really wanted to eat. Unfortunately, the supply was depleted, so I took fresh chicken breasts, cut them into small pieces, breaded them and baked them. I put them on Joel's plate and he asked, "What are these?" To which I replied, "Chicken Nuggets." "Oh," he remarked, taking a bite, "I don't like them." "Why?" I asked. And he said with a straight face, "They're too chicken-y!"

Cracked Up

Occasionally when I am speaking on the subject of mask-wearing, I have the opportunity to share this incident told me by my sister. We all know that part of aging is the wrinkles that somehow appear on our faces! I always rejoice that my sister has more wrinkles than I do, and talking about the importance of letting our true faces be seen, this story fits! She tells of her little granddaughter, cuddling on her lap, and reaching up to stroke her grandmother's face, announced, "I love you, Nana, even though your face is cracked!"

Position?

Our son loves practical jokes, and is brilliant at creating humor in almost any situation. I have always loved sharing this incident. He was dating a girl in high school, and he had arrived at her home to pick her up for a date. The family had a huge dog that could appear very threatening. As he rang the doorbell, he heard the deep-throated bark and growling of the dog, and the young lady's mother hollering "Back! Back." Anticipating, our son retreated to the gate and meekly asked, as the door opened, "Is this far enough?"

Sweet Aromas

For many years I have been uncomfortable in high-end retail stores. I guess I just felt that I didn't belong there, not being able to afford to buy anything. But I loved the perfume counter, and often would stand there sampling the scents on display. Trying to appear nonchalant and sophisticated, one day I took a few moments to find an intriguing aroma to try. I picked up my chosen bottle, and, throwing my head back and sniffing delicately, I pressed the pump several times. Not really smelling anything, I opened my eyes to discover that it was not perfume, but lotion, and it was visibly dripping down my new silk blouse! So much for appearing chic!!

Family Funnies

Shared by Tana and Bob Oldfield

Our granddaughter:

We were watching a video of all the grandchildren.

At four years old, her hair was long and curly. She pointed and tried to talk between her laughs, "That's when I was a **BOY!**"

We asked, "What do you mean? You're a girl."

"But I didn't have any hair, so I was still a boy."

We shook our heads. Now we knew. She always called babies who were bald, **"He!"**

———

One early weekend morning, she decided to make breakfast for her dolls and stuffed animals. She had a fairly new play kitchen. So far, so good!

But in a toddler's lack of good judgement, she used real eggs.

Trouble with a capital **T**!!

———

Our oldest son:

Our oldest son was about 5 when we were at a neighbor's Christmas party. Santa knocked on the door. When it was his turn to sit on Santa's lap, he told what he wanted for Christmas.

Then he looked up. "Santa, can I ask you a question?"

"Sure," Santa said.
"How is the progress of the *Alaska Pipeline* coming along?"
Santa was caught off guard!!

———

Youngest Son:

On the way to church one Sunday morning, our youngest son, just learning to talk, asked, "Who painted all the trees pink?"

———

Oldest Grandson:

Our shiny new car went in to the painter for some pinstriping.
    Grandson surprised, "Wow! What a great tattoo!"

———

    One December after kindergarten, while sitting at the kitchen counter, he looked up from his peanut butter cracker, "Grandma, is Santa real?"
    I turned the question around, "What do you think?"
    His eyes focused on the ceiling light, squint his eyes, pursed his lips, then announced, "I think for sure Santa is real, but I'm not so sure about those flying reindeers."

———

Oldest Grandson:

With his little face and the corners of his lips turned down, he slowly stated, "My neighbor's dog Scout died."

He hesitated, looked up and grinned, "Now I bet Scout's pooping in heaven!"

Youngest Grandson:

One fall day we were picking him up from school. He was walking down the sidewalk. A girl from his class suddenly ran up, hugged him and planted a kiss on his face.

As quickly as she came, she went running off to her grandma.

Pan-faced and stunned, he stared a look of *what was that all about*?

While treating my four-year-old grandson to the grocery store, I was bending over working hard to lug out a bag of sugar from the bottom shelf.

Suddenly I heard a loud: Grandma, do you know you have a big butt?

Blood Hounds

Chuck Lyon

In about 1936, when I was about ten or twelve, one of my buddies and I managed to get ourselves a job working for the local Sheriff's Department training blood hounds. Our training unit happened to be located in Lake City, WA, our home town. The hounds trained in the Lake City K-9 unit were well known, and highly respected. They were trained to capture escaped prisoners. Just possibly, they may have been occasionally recruited to aid search-and-rescue efforts…only a speculation on my part.

The way it worked is that an officer would take a couple of young boys who were looking for something exciting to do, take an item of clothing or something else each one had been holding, such as a book. They'd have each hound get the scent of each boy posing as an escapee. They gave the boys about a fifteen-minute head-start, with the intention that the boys would do everything they could think of to confuse the hounds.

The local Polo Cub was part of the training area. It should also be noted that not long previously, King County had created a clear-cut area by logging off a pretty good-sized piece of land in the vicinity. The trails were popular for hiking and horseback riding, Boy Scout Day outings, and sometimes BSA "overnighters." This added many more scents, and, therefore, many more ways to make the hounds have to work harder.

We "escapees" would run together for part of the time, then we'd separate onto differing trails, sometimes through scrub regrowth, sometimes through muddy paths...anything to be more of a challenge to the hounds.

I suspect that the officers probably didn't want to go out in foul weather, but there would be times when a previous rain would leave some of its "dirty work."

After a good workout, they'd take us and the hounds back to the kennel...us for our 50-cents each per run and the hounds for a good "feed."

A Fiery Wedding

Dean and Rose Gernon

The wedding of our youngest daughter's godmother was held at a venue located in the foothills of the San Gabriel Mountains above the San Fernando Valley. When we and all the guests arrived, we found fire trucks and a horde of firemen. The chief told us there was a brush fire above the place and that we couldn't go in there. We all went to a nearby park to wait for the all-clear. After about an hour it was decided to hold the ceremony there in the park. People went out and bought food and champagne. Just as things were starting, the chief came and said it was OK to go back to the venue.

So, we all trooped back and the wedding proceeded, complete with a bag piper! After the ceremony we all adjourned to the banquet hall. Just as we were being served, the fire chief rushed in and said the fire was out of control, burning towards the restaurant, and we had to evacuate NOW!!

In the parking lot, I paused long enough to photograph the fire and a helicopter refilling its water tank. Then we *drove out through a wall of flame*. Unfortunately, when the film was developed, I found the camera had malfunctioned and all the pictures were on top of each other in one frame.

In the mad dash, the wedding cake, (a beautiful multi-tier work of art made by the bride's uncle, who was a baker) was divided up. Some went with half the people to the bride's apartment, and the rest to the home of the bride's parents. We all had at least wedding cake, and the food at the restaurant went to the firemen.

That was the most exciting wedding we ever attended!

What is EMHE?

Carol and Connie Chapin

"Say that again!" My eyes bulged as I stared at Carol Chapin and slammed my fork to the table.

"Mary Jo, I have a story my daughter says is as exciting as winning the lottery! A little background first."

I took a big gulp of water as she continued.

"In 1963, my husband, Al, and I bought an old 100-year-old house in Kirkland, WA. We lived there with our 7 children and got our money's worth putting in a swimming pool. As our kids were growing up, we knew where they were and who their friends were…an easy way to keep an eye on them.

"Years later 1996, we sold the house to our oldest, Connie, who was 33 by that time. She had become a single mother of four in 2001."

As Carol continued, I had so many questions. We were talking recently, while she is a resident in Assisted Living and I and hubby Chris as independent living residents in Panorama Retirement in Lacey, WA.

Carol finally offered, "I tell you what, Mary Jo, why don't I get you in contact with Connie herself. Remember, I've introduced her to you? She will be able to answer your questions better."

Sure enough, her daughter Connie contacted me:

(I, Mary Jo Shaw, made a timeline nutshell for Connie's introductory information)

- 1996: at 33 yrs. old, Connie bought the house from her mom. Then 5 years later in
- 2001: Connie became a single mom of 4.
- 2002: at 38 yrs. old, Connie started Angelfish swimming to support self and family. Hired a nanny to pick up from school and take care of kids until 6 p.m. when Connie got out of the pool.
- 2007: event happened.

Connie picks up the story:

I taught swimming 6 years in the 100+year-old-house and pool.

Our family watched the show Extreme Makeover Home Edition (EMHE) every week. The kids and I wanted to apply, but thought we might as well buy a lottery ticket! My swim-families encouraged me the most, so I filled out the application and sent it in a year before they contacted me again. I also had all the families send in a letter of referral so just maybe we would stand out. A year later EMHE contacted us.

The event happened on September 26, 2007...the day we call the "door knock day," and we moved in on October 3, 2007

www.angelfishswimming.com

———

Her mother, Carol, continued her excitement with me.

Connie's kids begged their mom to write to the Extreme Home Makeover Home Edition program. They were accepted, and we saw the most beautiful and unique home with a backyard and *enclosed pool!*

The family was sent to Florida for the week in Disneyworld while the old 100+ year-old home was demolished and a new one was completed.

I remember the words MOVE THAT BUS. Connie was so overcome with joy, her knees buckled from underneath her. The children stood in awe with jaws dropped. The home is beautiful with pillars and large porch. Two dormers on the front upstairs.

In 2020 today, Connie says:

I am running the business with two instructors Miss Katie who has been teaching for 10 years with me and Miss Kristy (my sister) who has been teaching for a year with me.

Between the three of us we teach over 230 students every week.

My ultimate goal in teaching lessons is to save lives. Drowning has such a high rate of children deaths, and I want to do all I can to keep that from happening to anyone. All my graduates from swimming lessons can swim 5 different strokes and are safe in the water. This usually happens at around age 5 or 6. We are very proud to produce such young proficient swimmers.

———

I (Mary Jo Shaw) remembered viewing that program. Because it was so tense and the Washington rains were unforgiving, the usual 7 days of teardown-to-finish had to be extended an extra day. The video shows the dangerously unhealthy, rotten, dilapidating, asbestos-filled house. Many professional builders from all over came to push wheelbarrels through knee-deep watery mud and storm, etc.

The video inside the old house implies the family's love of God. Small and dilapidating as the rooms and halls were, a crucifix (a cross with the image of Jesus Christ) and photo of His mother Mary, were prominently displayed. The children's favorite posters, papers, pictures had their place, but didn't disturb a special area for the religious items.

Observing her deeply sincere, and emotional thanks to all workers, volunteers, and businesses, I was impressed that Connie felt comfortable taking her time to give the same sincere, loving, emotional gratitude to her Father God on national television. What a world, if we had more families such as the Chapins!

READER, I promise: you will be *very* unfortunate if you don't view or "review" again. Be ready!!

www.angelfishswimming.com

Virtuoso

Lois Williams

"...that the God of our Lord Jesus Christ, the Father of glory, may give unto you the spirit of wisdom and revelation in the knowledge of him; the eyes of your understanding being enlightened; that ye may know what is the hope of his calling, and what the riches of the glory of his inheritance in the saints."

The violinist,
a virtuoso.
Flying fingers expertly
form chords that are
made into music by the
long slow drawing of the bow
across the strings.
Mesmerized,
I watch the fascinating interplay,
my spirit absorbing
the beauty of the sound.

And then, truth sweetly dawns.
This is how God works in me.
Masterful omnipotent fingers
arrange, move, situate,
forming the chords that create music
as He draws His sovereign bow
across the strings of my life.

Reprinted by permission, from "Psalms From The Pathway",
Xulon Press © 2003 by Lois Williams
Email: fredlowill@msn.com

The Heat Sheet

Don Ulrich

In the spring of 2008, I introduced my second wife Ginny to her FIRST swim meet. As an avid swimmer all my life, I enjoyed swim meets, also as a past competitor. This meet was at the King County Aquatic Center in Federal Way. The pool seats about 2400 spectators. The meet was the Washington State High School Boys' Swimming Championships for 2008.

At the front door to the spectator seats, two men greeted us. I purchased our tickets from one of them. The other man asked Ginny, **"Would you like to buy a heat sheet?"**

Ginny look puzzled for many seconds before asking, **"Just how cold is it in there?"**

Startled, both men burst out laughing for several seconds. One announced, "I've never been asked that question before. Ask *him* (me) to explain."

I purchased a heat sheet and said I would explain just as soon as we sat down. We took our seats and I apologized to Ginny for *not* telling her what a heat sheet was *before* we came to the meet.

I explained, "A heat sheet is a program for the meet, *not* a blanket. For each event in this meet, there will probably be several heats. For example, say the pool has six numbered lanes and the event is the 100-yard backstroke with 24 entrants. Six swimmers will race each other at a time, in what is called a "heat." The heat sheet, i.e. program, would list each event and all its heats. For each heat, the program lists the swim-lane number, the boy's name, and high school.

Whew!

Oops!

Verl Rogers

We had a VW microbus in 1978. Our daughters were ten and twelve, and one night we drove to downtown Seattle for dinner at a fancy restaurant. Its name was "The Golden Coins" or something like it. I don't remember the restaurant well, but remember the parking. It smarts!

The VW was no great shakes as a vehicle. It was under-powered, top heavy, and the engine valves burned out too often. It had a three-speed gear shift. The engine was not meant for the heavy van, but for a regular sedan, so the rear wheels had reduction gears that forced the engine to run fast. The valve stems stretched and allowed the valves to burn. I had just paid a large sum to have new valves put in, so I had little patience with the blasted machine.

The whole deal soured me, so on top of my unusual opinion about the VW, a new item was added. On the other hand, my family loved the little van. It was handy for shopping, and it had a shelf behind the back seat where the girls could sit on carpet to view the world.

At the restaurant I found a parking place, but the space was small. The car in front was edged a foot or two farther back than it should. I squeezed in. The food was good, and we stayed inside for maybe an hour and a half.

When we came out, the car in front had not moved, but a new car behind ours had taken a few more inches of space toward my van. How was I to get out of that tight space?

I started the engine, released the hand brake, pressed the clutch down, and shifted into reverse. As I eased out the clutch, the rear bumper hit the bumper of the car behind. I said, "Oops!"

Giggles came from the back. Our daughters, full of restaurant food, thought the contact was funny. I pressed the clutch pedal and shifted into low gear. Again I let out the clutch slowly. The car moved forward until I hit the other bumper gently, but it still made noise. "Oops!" again. More giggles. More giggles became louder with each bump. Now I reversed the wheel, went forward until I hit another bump.

Full-scale laughter came from the back, and I heard a snort from my wife. She said that maybe I should quit saying "Oops," but voicing the sound helped.

Back and forth I went, little bumps front and back, with "Oops" and increasing laughter. I cranked the steering wheel and moved the rear end a few inches toward freedom. Finally, I got the van into the street and drove home.

Before I went into the house, I kicked a tire.

For months after, when one or the other would shout "Oops!" they would laugh.

Verl Rogers. Permission for print.

Snowed In Nome, Alaska!

Carol Severson

I went to open the door and about three feet of snow had blown and packed across the front and back doors. I couldn't get out. My heart pounded.

That's how my day started a little over a year after my husband Don retired. We had moved to Nome, Alaska, to be interim managers of a Christian radio station. We lived in the former managers' home, and every winter the snow would drift and pack against the doors making it impossible to shovel from the inside of the house.

Most mornings Don would go to the station ahead of me. I'd show up about an hour later to manage the office.

With this mound of snow on the other side of both doors, I picked up the phone, "DON! We've never had snow this deep. I can't open the doors to get out."

His voice shivered a bit, "What a predicament! Chuck's already here, too. We will come to see what we can do. Stay warm, Carol!"

You won't believe…the two men dug a tunnel. I actually crawled out through that tunnel, nudging our little dog Daisy to keep moving ahead me. That snow-tunnel was packed so hard, that later that day Don carved out steps so we could walk **DOWN** and **INTO** the doorway to the house. He grew up in North Dakota and was used to wind-packed snow.

One of several unusual experiences in the frozen North!

Three Childhood Favs

Sarah Shaw

My granddaughter Sarah Shaw, age 16 in 2020, shares...

Granny, I have one!

Remember that time when we were at the YMCA of the Rockies in Estes Park for a week? I was a little over 3 ½ and Emily was only 18 months. In the craft building, she was painting her ceramic unicorn and kept insisting that she needed to cover up *each of the entire layers* of paint with a different color? She eventually painted the whole thing magenta. Well, she still has that unicorn! Remember all of the good naps and picnics that we had throughout that week with just the three of us...you, Emily and me?

And remember all of the times we would walk on the greenbelt behind your Las Vegas home? We'd collect pine cones to use making crafts...and sometimes we'd pack a lunch basket and have a picnic on the greenbelt tables.

There was another time that we arrived from Leander (Texas) to you in Las Vegas. The moment I stepped inside the front door, I asked, "Granny Jo, can we do crafts?" My family laughed, and you bent over with a big smile and said, "Oh, Sarah, that will be fun. It's *two o'clock in the morning*. Let's get some sleep, and we'll do it first thing in the morning." Man, I was sleepy!

(Yes, Sarah, I will always cherish those memories, and it warms my heart that you still remember them, too!)

As I, Granny Jo (author, Mary Jo Shaw) received Sarah and Emily's stories, I recalled on the same trip to our home in Las Vegas (when the girls, about ages 2 and 4) played "school" in our breakfast area. Sarah transformed into the teacher role. Emily morphed into a student with her eyes glued to Teacher Sarah...as did several dolls in a semicircle sitting on the small children's chairs. Some stuffed animals perched on the kitchen table chairs. (Granny's insert: don't all grandparents have little tables and chairs for their visiting little angels?) Sarah parked herself on a tall stool *facing the class,* reading the story of Adam and Eve from the children's Bible story book. My ears perked up when she interjected her *teacher comment* at the slow pace of a four-year old. "That's...good...Eve. You ate the apple al-l-l up."

Two Shorts

1. Weather Here Is Always Different

Verl Rogers

First it fogged and then it blew
Then it friz and then it snew.
Then it thew and rain came thru
With sleet, then fog, then sky of blue.
But very shortly after then,
It friz and blew and snew agin.

Verl Rogers. Permission to print.

2. Child in a Tub

Verl Rogers

Soap, soap, soap and towel,
Towel and water please,
For billowy billowy billowy suds,
To scrub your dirty knees.

Verl Rogers. Permission to print.

Dad Waters Garden

Understandably anonymous.

It's the *shortest story* in this book!

At first, I thought Dad was watering the garden!

Seats I've Sat In

Evelyn Peterson

I'm 93 years old. I'm in my room alone on September 30, 2020, during Covid-19. I'm legally blind. I'm counting my blessings from a long life. I love to call every couple of weeks to laugh with Mary Jo Shaw, whose husband, Chris, is my first cousin. So…I did today.

Here is our conversation as written by Mary Jo:

"Evelyn," I asked, "what did you do lately to entertain yourself?"

"Oh, Mary Jo, so glad you asked. I was counting how many *unusual seats I've sat in* around the world."

Immediately Evelyn began rattling off a list, non-stop, seeming not to take a breath. My head was spinning. I thought she was joking.

"Whoa! Evelyn, slow down! I'm lying down and I want to get a piece of paper from my side table." I did, and laid my iPhone on my chest so I could write. "Evelyn, I want you to start over. Okay to put this in my Goofies and Goodies book I'm writing?"

Evelyn laughed, "Oh that would be fun!" She started over:

I've sat on a seat in the Goodyear Blimp.

Sat on an army tank in North Fort Hood, Texas.

Sat on a bench seat in a rickshaw one Saturday night, racing with my good friend Betty who was in another rickshaw. (Reader: a rickshaw is a small, two-wheeled, cart-like passenger vehicle with a fold-down top, pulled by one hired person, formerly used widely in Japan and China.)

Sat on a seat on the Concorde from Heathrow Airport in London to JFK in New York, arriving in only 3 hours/18 minutes.

Sat in a fighter plane from Edwards Air Force Base in California...

I sat in the seat of a machine that spun pilots to test how many G's they could handle. (I didn't spin, but I did sit!)

A double decker bus in England.

"Hey, wait, wait, Evelyn!" I interrupted, "I have to get another piece of paper. What experiences!"

On cue, Evelyn went right on between my *Oh's* and *Oh No's*!

I rode an elephant in Bangkok, Thailand...

Sat on the top of a camel in North Africa in corduroy jeans that stunk to the high heavens.

Sat on a seat in a boat trip down the Blue Danube from Budapest, Hungary to France.

I sat in my Cessna 150 pilot seat. We teased that its motor felt and sounded like a sewing machine motor. I eventually flew wide miles over cities in Texas. Oh, Mary Jo, I'd fly over New Braunfels High School. The students would point up and say, "That little plane looks and sounds like it's having trouble." My two girls, Faye Lynn and Francie who were students there, would say, "No, that's my mom just letting me know it's her!"

Then there was a seat during the annual weeklong *Fiesta San Antonio* Friday night's river parade in the 60's—riding on the float representing the local TB Hospital.

Finally, Evelyn reminded me that she initially met me in Taipei, Taiwan.

For you, reader, Mary Jo must interject here. My husband, Chris, worked for Braniff International Airlines. We could ask for unlimited, absolutely free passes—always first class—anywhere in the world with 50% off the plush hotels as long as he showed up for work. On one trip, we had flown to Hawaii, China, Hong Kong, Japan,

Australia, and Indonesia. On a whim Chris suggested, "Oh, I have a first cousin whose husband is stationed in Taiwan. I'll call her from here. She'll put us up a few nights. She is very sweet, she'd love you, and you'd love her!"

"Chris, no way. We can't just call at the last minute and invite ourselves. You were a bachelor for 38 years, dropping in on people. Remember when we 'dropped in" on Bohn and Sue at night on our first date? You kept ringing the doorbell until Bohn peeked through the barely opened door whispering, "Oh, hi, Chris, so good to see you! Sue just came home from the hospital this afternoon. We had a baby boy! Imagine me coaching my own son in football games." They let us in and visited politely with us..."

"Oh, Mary Jo, Evelyn would just love for us to come." And Chris was right. That's when I met his cousin Evelyn.

Evelyn now refreshed my mind of a *special seat* we all sat in when in Taiwan. "Remember when I drove you to look over the China Sea to the mainland of China? We were on a high incline overlooking a large grassy area. In the middle of that area, was a ten-foot stone watch tower. The stones had little spaces for soldier army guards to see through. We weren't supposed to stop there, or even slow down, but you couldn't see the little openings, unless I pointed them out to you. I paused the car a few seconds."

We strained to see those little openings. Suddenly an armed Taiwanese armguard appeared and bent over to observe the three of us inside the car. Then he studied the car's diplomatic license plate, and instantly stood tall at attention and saluted toward Evelyn in the *car's seat*.

We headed to downtown Taipei to observe the Federal building. As we slowed to listen to Evelyn's guided tour comments, army soldiers again approached us with guns. Twice in one day!

"You know, Mary Jo, I've traveled a total of 41 countries, but by far, our United States of America is the best place God could have allowed for me to live on this earth." (Amen, Evelyn!)

I told her, "I want to write about your many other unique, unusual, funny experiences into another story. God bless again. I love you."

NOTE:

Before beginning this story, I Googled on my iPhone the "distance between Buda and Pest," expecting the very short distance over the Danube River, right? Here's what I got:

A very beautiful, clear, colorful map of the USA, with a blue line between two points:

*A nice circle on the point in southeast—**BUDA**, Texas. A blue line was drawn to the upper northwest USA and a perfect circle indicated: Washington **PEST** Services and Consultants. 2,178 miles, via I-84.*

Depths of Denial

Anonymous #2

I usually try to leave the country so nobody can wish me a happy birthday. On several occasions, I've spent it underwater…so someone would have to learn scuba and sign language to be able to wish me a happy birthday!

Smellavision Memories

LeNoi Steckley

A smell to remember! My brother-in-law worked for a meat packing company in Omaha. He took us on a tour. After they kill the pigs, the entire pigs are dumped into a huge tank of boiling hot water. It spins them around so fast, it removes the hair. The pigs are hung upside down by their back legs, then split down the front so the entrails can hang out for easy removal.

To this day when I eat pork, I remember that smell so vividly, that it's hard to eat pork.

My eyes still envision the bubbling hot water, and my nose hairs still retain that stinky, nasty pig hair!

Convent to Catwalk ... Writing My Story

Mary Jo Shaw

Why at age 16 would I enter a religious convent, stay 13 years, leave, and immediately be trained to model for the greatest designers in the world?

Before we moved to Panorama Retirement in 2011, my family and friends knew most of the answers to those questions, coaxing me to write my unusual stories. I always loved to write, and won first-prize in two different poem contests...a whopping $15 for each. A lot of money in the 50s, especially to a child!

English was my favorite class from early elementary through college. I wanted to major in English, but dreaded the prospect of straining in a college library studying references, Shakespeare, writing papers with footnotes, etc. And to actually teach all that as a profession as a religious nun...my insides still quiver at that thought! But why?

Diagramming was my friend and forte. In tenth grade whenever Sister English teacher handed out one of her lengthy pre-prepared sentences as punishment for talking in class, I volunteered the *socially gifted* classmates to let me do their diagrams. The cost? A few sheets of the necessary three-ring binder papers required to tape at points to complete the diagram.

In the 1950s in the convent, we were assigned our majors. The day of our college English entrance placement exams, I trembled. If I did **well**, I'd be in the advanced class and probably end up teaching English. Drats! My plan?

After Sister Monitor distributed the exam booklets (and gave the simple you-may-begin) she floated on Cloud9 with *The Iliad and the Odyssey* for the next hour. Girls bent over cautiously studying the pages. I flipped page after page, easily filling in the small Easter eggs with my #2 pencil. Then I panicked! Only two more pages to go. My heart pounded so fast, my arm jerked.

My thoughts blared. *STOP! What are you doing, Mary Jo? You're used to rapid responses in grammar class. STOP!*

I gulped. *I've gotta go back to mark some answers incorrect and leave some of 'em blank!! How many should I do?*

My eraser worked fast.

Weird! *Oh, God, am I cheating?!* My head assumed the same position of the girls slaving to fill in the right bubbles. I could not imprison myself in library stacks AND also have time to expand my God-given music talent. I'd rip myself apart with the pull to do both.

However, I didn't want to wind up a lying nun, either. I was content.

As a child I hated to read...after interpreting each sentence or paragraph several times, I'd forget it the next day. Dyslexia doesn't desire dissipating (even now at age 81)!

On my first mission in the convent, I asked to teach grammar and diagraming to provide office-work time for the assistant principal/English teacher. A win-win!

By the time we retired to Panorama, I was questioning what to do with all the unusual experiences stacked between the bookends of my life.

Eventually I tiptoed into a free Write Your Life class. Facilitator Charlotte and the other six residents offered me a seat around a large table.

Edith began reading her next episode as a vicar's wife in the 1930s.

Their move into the two-story, small vintage parsonage happened on the identical stormy snow-day as the transferring vicar was moving out. Moving both families in and out on the same day saved the transporters time and money—it was the depression. However, both families had small children, and it was lunchtime!! Hungry kids, confusion of belongings, packed glass-kitchenware, no paper plates, no microwave...

In our writing class, we each simply read about 10 minutes, with no constructive comments.

My jaw dropped when I pictured my elderly resident friends in their missions as fighter pilots in WWII, Vietnam, or Korea...one as a prisoner of war. Others were teachers, politicians, farm wives. I always had plenty to write. If we had had no time to compose, we attended just to enjoy the ongoing stories. I laugh inside now: I'd never allowed myself to become addicted to soap operas!

The style of one resident impressed me with use of conversations, scenes and grounding. He stunned <u>me</u> with his encouragement, "Mary Jo, you need to write your stories in a book."

Whoa! I AM retired. I have time! Never thought I'd write a book! But I hungered for critiques.

About a year later, I showed up to the PanWriters' class. Internationally known playwright Bryan Willis, taught three writing classes on campus for a small fee. (Today he adds screenwriting.) I read two pages of *My Wedding Nightmare*, and left that first day with swollen encouragement from Bryan and the nine student residents.

We wrote from a prompt, read aloud from copies made for each student, and offered constructive critiques! Bryan passed out books on writing, to borrow or keep.

After about a year, author Patricia Swan moved into our neighborhood and joined our class. Her first story proved she had experience in writing! After walking home together, Patricia asked, "Mary Jo, would you lend me some of your stories to critique for you?"

"WOW, thank you!" I dashed into my garden home, grabbed some pages from a 3-ring binder, and shoved them into Patricia's opened chair-walker.

Putting toward home, she turned, "I'll call you over when I've finished. We'll talk about the papers." That began 4 ½ years of weekly volunteer-mentoring, with her gentle demands to read and study books on writing, and improving. What a blessed feeling!

I continued in Bryan's class until time to write about the years of my life as a nun, and then as a high fashion model. **I firmly wanted those careers kept a secret here in Washington until after printing.** I didn't want to read that section aloud, so I dropped the class to spend time writing.

Besides my family, I entrusted only two people with my secret: Bryan, who accepted to be my editor, and Patricia, my mentor. "If anyone else finds out, I'll know one of you or my husband, Chris, squealed. Don't even mention the title, *Convent to Catwalk*. That will give it away!" I wanted the careers to be a surprise.

Just about every resident knew I was writing a book, but they begged to know "just" the title!

After 5 ½ years of writing four to twelve hours daily, I finished pounding my exhausted laptop until letters on the keys forced the seek-and-you-shall-find method of typing. And I should have taken stock in printer-paper!

With encouragement from Bryan Willis and his professional substitutes, I braved up to **self-print** *Convent to Catwalk* with 65 pictures! Self-published, I'm my own boss.

I am blessed with the explosion and constant excitement of my family book. It had spread to six states the first month, with reorders for gift giving.

I love book reviews/signings with Q/A at churches, clubs, organizations, luncheons, and donating part proceeds, if they are fundraising.

For me, writing is recreation, not work. I thank God for 55 years of teaching music, volunteering piano-playing on our campus, and sharing His gift to write.

The more I thank God, the more blessings He gives...far over and beyond!

High Rise and Hot

Jean Garwood

Managing high rise office buildings in Los Angeles offers many exasperating and unusual challenges. My mind refuses to forget some of the events. My top stories of those high rises are the times they lost air conditioning. During heat waves in Southern California, A/C repair trucks, racing from one client to the next, produced the only cool ripples in the air. We couldn't do anything, so we were at the mercy of our maintenance company to fix the unit as quickly as possible. We'd have the unit airlifted from the building by helicopter.

Since windows in these buildings could not be opened, the offices became hot boxes. Tenants would keep calling and blaming management, "It's too hot to do business." I would use all of my people skills to communicate with and listen to my upset tenants.

One time the air conditioning had gone out in the penthouse. That large group of tenants were LA lawyers (not the most flexible people)! As I sat in my office, a male tenant from the penthouse arrived at the door wearing black bikini underwear and smoking a cigar. He announced, "This is *my* response to the heat."

I *should* have told that lawyer, "We do not allow solicitors in our building!"

Another time, after searching my brain, I called the owner, "May I have an ice cream party in that location in the building that *still* has A/C? It would be a nice distraction from the heat and no air-conditioning!"

"No, let's wait until it's all over." That was that!

Buzz…Buzz…Buzz… I slammed the phone into it's cradle. I dressed into my strawberry ice cream colored dress and marched straight to the store.

The sign I made on my door had the familiar, "When we're given lemons, we make lemonade." That was the invitation for everyone to come in and have ice cream. Beaming from ear to ear, I spent the day dishing up ice cream for all the happy faces!

Long Short Steps

Margaret A.

Note: On the first day of the school year 2020, my *baby* sister, Margaret (Peggy) sent this during Covid's stay-at-home restrictions. At age 17, William was starting online senior classes:

This morning I took William by the hand and walked him from the hallway to his study room. "There, I walked you to school. We've never gotten to do that before!!"

He just laughed, hugged and kissed me.

"Thanks, Geegee! Boy, that wore me out!!"

Sedate Enjoyment

Verl Rogers

The world is new to small children. One mother said, "My one-year-old grows so fast, sometimes I have trouble. One day I gave her brussels sprouts to eat, and the next day she asked for them. It took me a while to find that she was saying "sprouts."

One day I came home from work to find that our Susan, age three, and baby Nancy, age one, were sitting in the little red wagon of Jerry-next-door. Jerry was pulling them around the yard, and they were all three looking unusually quiet and sedate.

I went in to find my wife and she asked, "Are those kids doing anything?" I told her how they seemed to be satisfied with an ordinary wagon ride.

Janet went to the window and looked. "Oh yes, they are changing fast. I haven't seen them riding before, but that's new. They must like it a lot, just going round and round."

Yes, riding in a red wagon was something new to their world, and it brought a quiet joy.

That event with the wagon took place in—let's see—1959. We moved away in 1965, the last time we saw Jerry. Would he then in 1965 want to give our girls a ride in a little red wagon? Memories please me. That ride was a peaceful and pleasant event.

Verl Roger. July 5, 2020. Printed with permission.

The Record Quarter Mile

Tom Allen

"Where'd you get that watch, Gene?"

"Oh, it's no ordinary watch. It's a stop watch." The first click started it, the second click showed the lapsed time, and the third click put it back to zero.

"Amazing, what shall we do with it?"

"We need to time something." After some deep thought and investigation, we discovered that the block next to Gene's house was almost exactly a quarter mile around.

"Let's race!"

Most was sidewalk, but the short sides forced us out into the street.

"Watch out for cars."

I don't remember ever racing against each other. We only raced one at a time against the stop watch.

"Okay, Gene. It's your turn. I'll hold the watch."

The only problem along the route was this Boston Bulldog that lives about 100 yards from the finish line. He would charge out from the back yard and chase the runner for several lot lengths.

"BARK! BARK! BARK!"

"Runners to your mark! Get set, GO!"

CLICK!. Off Gene dashes. A little over a half a minute later, he appears around the far corner, head held back, mouth open, knees pumping.

I glance at the watch. "HURRY!"

Gene tried harder. "I'm going as fast as I can."

Another two lots and out comes the dog, barking and running along the grass close to Gene's heels.

"**YARP!**" The dog runs head first into the telephone pole.

I laugh. "Serves him right."

Gene glances back at the dog. The dog rocks back, shakes his head, bares his teeth and takes off after Gene, knowing full well that Gene had clobbered him. What astonishing speed! You never saw such a sprint to the finish line. Both were a blur. Gene broke our old speed record as they roared past the finish line, around the corner and out of sight!

The dog wouldn't open his mouth. Gene wouldn't close his, "**OW!OW!OW!**

Two Teacher Stories

Patrick Osborn

#1. Science Answer

During my first year of teaching, one of the girls (I had all girls that year—Bishop Lynch HS had the boys on one side of the building, girls on the other) cautiously raised her hand and said, "Mr. Osborn, some of us were talking. We think that when we ask you how something scientific works, maybe you just make up something. We don't think you could *know* so much about *how* so many things work.

I laughed out loud and told her that if I didn't know something, I certainly would admit it. "I've always liked to know *how* things work, and I studied science for years. I read Popular Science cover to cover each month. So…I often know the answers to science related questions."

I always smile about that.

Author Mary Jo Shaw's comment:

My sister Jerri and I babysat Patrick before we were teenagers. Yes, when Patrick was still learning to be firm on his little feet, before his mom (our Aunt Nancy) left the house, her *only* last-minute comment warned, "Girls, be *sure* to keep Patrick from examining how the electric wall-plugs and lamp-sockets work."

His grandfather, George Hofmann, built a wooden box about 26 x 18 inches, and 6 inches deep. Out of the hinged-lid top protruded a light bulb with a switch, another one with a pull chain, a door bell, a large buttoned buzzer...seems a few other objects, too. The batteries and wires lived inside that prized box. A sturdy pad lock hung on the front.

Patrick sat on the hard-wood floors hours manipulating that treasured chest. Batteries needed to be changed *more* often than planned. However, he'd try to *repair* the gadget by pulling or pushing harder. We knew his investigating mind would guide him onto scientific roads somewhere. Sure enough! Thanks for the memory, Patrick.

#2. Visual Acuity

Each year in science class, when we got to the segment on visual acuity, I would work my way to the **back** of the room and lean against the back wall and say, "From where I am standing, you should be able to read the large red numbers on the periodic table (the atomic number) at the front of the room."

Their eyes would study the chart.

I told them, "I never had a vision screening till I was in ninth grade. If I had had glasses *before then,* I probably would be a genius by now!" That always got a laugh.

One year when I said they should be able to read those large red numbers, a girl in the *middle* of the classroom blurted out loudly, "NO WAY!!!!!"

God Blessed America in Gentle Care

Mary Jo Shaw

When I reached from the piano bench to recoup a sheet of music from the floor, it yelled, "Play me next!"

I was *ending* my twice-a-month volunteering of piano entertainment for about twenty residents in our Panorama's Gentle Care (for those with dementia and Alzheimer's). They were finishing their cookies and juice in the day room. I held the piece of music above my head, "We need God's blessing on America, so I will now play *God Bless America*. You may simply listen, sing, hum, or pray the song."

As the first note sounded, a fragile gentleman in the back of the room stood as tall as his fragile body allowed. His quivering fingers reached for his cap, which he held gently against his thin chest. With his head bowed in deep devotion, he lowered his eyelids.

I wondered whether the faint hum floating from others around the room was generated from him.

Finally, the ending, "...A-me-ri-ca, my ho-me, sweeeet ho-me." The gentleman replaced his cap, wiped a tear, and struggled to take his seat.

Everyone was silent. I continued to gather my music books, but looked up and raised my voice. "Thank you, sir. Thank you for standing for the playing of *God Bless America*. We appreciate your respect to this patriotic prayer, and it's not even the *Star-Spangled Banner*."

Betty in charge of the entertainment reiterated, "Yes, John, thank you."

I pat my good-byes on each resident's shoulder and lastly to the veteran.

"Thank you again for your service to keep our country safe." Asking him questions, we learned that he had flown bomber-missions in WWII. I was admiring one of the last of a few heroes in America from that era.

I emphasized, "We can't let our grandchildren, greatgrandchildren and future generations ever forget those horrible years. I notice the tiny little gold wings on your cap."

He nodded his head and pointed to his friend in a wheeled chair to his left, "This my buddy, Joe. He served in the Air Force, too."

Recognizing his friend's Veteran Cap, I bent down, "I see you have your wings, too! Thank you, sir. We deeply appreciate your service. We can't imagine what you two went through to keep us safe. God bless you."

As I returned down the first floor of our Convalescent/Rehab Center, I prayed, "Lord God, I place all veterans into Your hands. Help me not ever take them for granted. Please bless our country, despite many times of forgetting You in our daily lives. We have so much for which to be thankful."

God had blessed a part of America in Gentle Care with a reminder...from two dedicated veterans.

Easy As Pie

Verl Rogers

My mother made pies all the time, and they were all good. Then I became engaged to marry Janet and ate pie at Janet's house. Janet's mother made better pies than my mother, though I kept quiet on the subject of comparisons. It is good politics for a pie eater to congratulate the cook for any pie, otherwise you'll never get a second helping.

Then Janet and I married, and Janet made good pies, though I never said what I thought...that her mother's pies were better! Again, I took care to thank the cook for any pie. It was always a pleasure to visit Mother Bixler and find she had made a pie for us.

In time, we had two baby girls who grew up to become good cooks like their mother, and both Sue and Nancy learned to make pies. From the start, Sue made better pies than her sister or her mother. Then Sue went off to attend Wenatchee Valley College for a year, and to live with Grandmother Bixler just 12 miles away, in Cashmere. The two of them were delighted to live together, and Grandma taught Sue how she made pies. Sue improved!

On a family visit to Grandma's, in the kitchen, Janet watched the two make pies together. She reported to me later, "It was strange to see how careless, almost sloppy, they were to throw those two pies together! Can't tell you just what they did, but they worked fast. We have plenty of last year's huckleberries in the freezer at home. Any time you want pie from now on, give Sue some of those berries and ask. She's even better than Mother."

Recently I spoke with my friend Jeannie about piemaking, and she said, "Oh yes, I go fast too; my hands just flow. Once when I was making a pie, my sister in the kitchen said, 'Stop, what did you just do?' I replied, I dunno. If I stop to think, I can't do it."

A few years went by, Sue married Jay and they set up housekeeping together. Early in the marriage, Jay found that Sue's pies were outstanding and on one visit he mentioned the fact to me.

I told him, "Yes, it's easy for her. Have you read the instructions—not just the recipe, but the whole routine—needed to make a pie? You've got to mix up the dough, then refrigerate it, then roll out the crust, put it in the pan, chill the dough again, prepare the filling, fill the pie, roll out the top crust, crimp the edges, brush the crust with egg yolk, cut steam vents, bake very hot for a time, then reduce the heat and finish baking, then let the thing cool four hours and fight off the men in the meantime. It's a surprise to me that anyone can make any kind of pie, but Sue makes the whole thing seem easy."

At the next opportunity, I dug two jars of huckleberries out of the freezer and handed them to Sue, asking for two pies. You see, there were five of us in the house that weekend, and one pie would not go far enough. Jay and I agreed; his wife (my daughter Sue) was a magical pie maker.

On the other hand, it helps to have a supply of pie-making fruit on hand. For years, Janet and I would make a summer-trip for huckleberries, bringing home a couple of gallons of the wild fruit, which we froze. Apples are always to be had at the store, but peaches have to be canned at harvest, or frozen. We bought two flats of strawberries in season and froze them, and froze a supply of rhubarb as well.

Verl Rogers. Printed with permission.

Battle of the Alamo and Coronavirus

Rosemary Geyer, San Antonio, Texas

I was just thinking about the Coronavirus and how many people are dying. Sometimes we begin to become depressed.

Today I thought about my great-great-grandmother who lost her husband, aunt, uncle, cousin and her cousins' two children to cholera in 1833. She was Juana Perez Alsbury, and her child was my great-grandfather Alejos. When Alejos was 18 months old, his mother Juana was taken to the Alamo by Jim Bowie who was ill, possibly with yellow fever that was going around. Cholera was also rampant.

Juana's cousin Ursala Veramendi was married to Jim Bowie. Bowie played a prominent role in the Texas Revolution, culminating in his death during the defense at the Battle of the Alamo. He fought along with Davy Crockett.

Despite the cholera and yellow fever which hovered over the Battle of the Alamo, Juana and the other women and children survived the diseases and the Battle.

Those women never gave up. Neither will we give up our battle with this COVID-19 virus. We will do our best efforts as if it all depended on us, and pray as if it all depended on God.

Peace,

Rosemary Geyer

Whatta Wedding With Warren!

Judy Horton

Warren was 15 years older than I was. I knew his mom, dad, and Warren's older brother, Larry, who was 10 years older than I was. I also knew his wife, Alice and their four children. We were members of the same Lutheran Church in Santa Monica. My first husband and three daughters left Santa Monica in 1972 for Fountain Valley, Orange Country, Calif. We were there until (22 years divorced) I moved back to Santa Monica.

It is now 1994 and Warren's wife had died in 1992. It is Father's Day. As we were walking out of church, I asked Warren where he was going for Father's Day Dinner.

He surprised me, "My kids are all busy. How about you joining me for dinner?" He being 15 years older, I hesitated, but *I accepted.*

We started going places together. In July he asked me to accompany him at his daughter's wedding. Again, he surprised me, "Will you marry me?" (I was currently seeing two other fellas!) He offered me a very good life. He would take care of me financially, and I would take care of him with companionship. Again, *I accepted.*

Monday *prior* to our wedding day, my oldest daughter, Susan, arrived from Washington with husband and three daughters. Susan's husband, a Lutheran pastor, was to be part of the wedding ceremony. We adults had a dinner at church, as our Bishop was visiting congregations in our Synod.

When we arrived back home, youngest granddaughter, Jenny, had vomited in one of my sleeping bags. Come Wednesday, middle granddaughter, Molly vomited in a sleeping bag.

Friday, my youngest daughter, Melinda and her husband arrived from Colorado. My middle daughter, Pamela, lived near Disneyland, and so Melinda, Susan and their families all met there. They all came back to *our* home to spend the night and stay until after the wedding.

I awoke about 1:00 am or so, to oldest granddaughter standing in my bathroom vomiting. I tried to get her into the shower, as it was in her long hair. She was fighting me, so her mom came in to take over. I went back to bed. At 4:00 am, I woke up and had to vomit. At 5:00 am, I heard Warren in bathroom...he threw up. This is now Saturday. Luckily, most of the wedding plans had been accomplished for tomorrow.

We both stayed in our beds. I directed things from there and the kids took over. Warren and I ate soda crackers and sipped 7UP all day and evening. Ladies that were to work our reception at our home called to say they also had the flu, and can they send their young daughters? One of our soloists called, she was in Wyoming, her dad had brain surgery...she would try to get home in time. Saturday, late evening my son-in-law started vomiting.

Sunday morning, those who were well went to church. My pianist called she had the flu, but she said our choir director will fill in. I said this was fine- tell him to watch for my signal when to stop playing prior to the starting of the ceremony.

As I was taking care of my hair, my stepsister came in to greet me. I was talking and started spraying my hair... with *water instead of my hairspray*. Oh Well!! Needless to say—sleeping bags found their way into the trash!

We all arrived at church with time to welcome many friends. We had sent out 400 invitations. Guests came from my church in Fountain Valley, some from out of state and others from *this* church.

I asked my friends to bring an appetizer…Warren wouldn't ask his friends.

While planning our wedding, I asked photographer not to position my mom and dad close in pictures. They had been divorced for over 25 years. The day of the wedding, I came out to the church entrance to greet friends, and there were the three of them…mom, dad and his new girlfriend in conversation. So much for distancing!

Warren was not feeling great, so we sat in the first pew up front. It was 3:00 pm. No pastor!! Music played on (and my soloist did get back from Wyoming.)

But still no pastor. About 3:10 pm he arrived. He was getting sick!! My son-in-law was still not feeling well…he couldn't wear his robe as pastor (too hot), so he sang in shirt and tie. Thinking positively, things were going well.

Time for the big ceremony! Warren announced for everyone who is, or ever was, related to Warren and me—born into or by marriage—to please come up and join us at the altar while we repeated our vows. It was so beautiful. We all crowded around. Afterward, while everyone was still at the altar, I asked for the photographer to take a picture of all of us. I counted them later—over 50 people!! (**Now, years later during our Covid-19 in 2020, I grin: so much for *distancing*!!**)

Warren had announced to guests, "Please leave cars in the church parking lot and walk to our home. We're two blocks away, and there's better parking here at church. Please start the reception, and we'll join you after we take a few more pictures."

Warren's son met us in the front yard, announcing, **"We are all out of wine!!"**

It couldn't be! It was a *wine-fountain flowing*. The young girls had put *beer tumblers* by the wine fountain. His son flew off to the store. There were well over 200 people at our home!

We had some great food! I had said "no personal gifts" (combining two households was already too much stuff). We did ask them to bring food items for local food bank. So much food came—some wrapped as wedding gifts. My friend delivered over 200 pounds (and gift certificates) to the local food bank. He had to make 2 trips.

The "family jokesters" took all of my dry macaroni and scattered it inside and outside the car. Macaroni in the glove compartment, ashtrays, under and between the seats, the floor and back window. Then they proceeded to blow up all of my plastic bags and stuff them inside the car. (When we sold the car 2 years later, macaroni still appeared in some places!)

This is the 26th of February and, of course, it rained that night. We had tented the backyard and had tiki torches if it rained. We spent the night in a local hotel. Our car had soggy (appearing cooked!) macaroni all over its exterior.

We had a BBQ the *next weekend* for family and friends to thank them all. We had to drink up the beer keg that people didn't realize was farther back in the yard.

Through all of the unplanned happenings that occurred, Warren and I didn't panic or get upset. This was a wonderful time in our lives.

Added notes: On Saturday night at dinner, (Warren and I were not there) his daughter, Donna asked Warren's children Dianna, Doug and David, along with my children and grandchildren, to go around the room and say why the two of us should get married. Donna put it all to together and shared it during the ceremony.

I have to preface the next incident with some information. Before I moved back to Santa Monica, I traveled 43 miles away Monday through Friday for my job, so I stayed with my brother or with friends who put me up in in their homes during that time. I was living out of my suitcase. On the weekends, I traveled back to my apartment to do necessary things there, then I hit the road again for another Monday through Friday. **I felt like a bag-lady! (This is why Susan said, "… and now she can unpack—she is home.)**

At the ceremony Susan wanted to share her thoughts. She couldn't get her words out without blubbering. She finally said, "My mom is home now, and she can finally unpack her bags."

Donna was next to share thoughts, "How can I follow that?" Everybody laughed!

Both Warren and I agreed that What Ever Will Be Will Be. This is the way God planned it. We think He got a Good Laugh!!!!!

I have not included everything that occurred during this time. Believe you me, there were other things!

I have told my story to many people. However, I have never written it down until now. I got a chuckle while writing this, and it will be put in a place for my family to read. I might add the things left out of this story!!

No "Trespassing" Fun Aging Fig Tree's Confession

Jerri Kay

When I was a child and saw a sign that said *NO TRESPASSING*, I thought that's what they were talking about in the prayer *Our Father!*

Unfortunately, I had to go to the DMV today. The lines were gross (but my license had expired). A gentleman came up to me and said, "Miss, this line is for seniors over 60."

I asked, "Do you have one for over eighty? I'm tired."

Everybody laughed. I have fun with my age!

I remember the time when I was seven years old, and we had to go to confession every Friday. I would make up sins because I didn't know what to tell the priest. So, one time I told him I committed adultery. He took a big gasp and laughed so hard, I almost ran out of the confessional! I thought it was *adult/tree*! We always climbed in the big fig tree on University Street.

Humorous Friend's Hope

Mary Jo Shaw

While observing this COVID-19 stay at home, I keep reviewing the huge stack of piano pieces I've been playing all over the campus so often. I know from experience that if I don't, I'll be re-teaching myself. Dyslexia definitely doesn't do that without difficulty. I **teach myself pieces** I've always wanted to learn, but didn't have time to do.

Hubby Chris, in his recliner and remote, is backed up to my electronic-piano's chair. I hear the news, Gomer Pyle, Carol Burnett, or Bible preachers, as I play with low volume, and no headset. Actually, I can still focus on my piano and improve each day. I've discovered *that late night practice* helps me focus and retain if I go to bed right away after practicing.

My always uplifting, humorous friend, just emailed me, "I just hope when this stay-at-home is over, and you play the new pieces of music all over your Panorama campus, you don't start speaking the news reports at the same time!"

Death Is Close

Verl Rogers

I hope this essay is not morbid, but at age 93, I would not be surprised to wake up dead or dying tomorrow. A patient down the hall is 100, and we have several others in the nursing home who are older than I. They are thoroughly alive, so my age is not unusual. The longevity table says, on average, I have about 3.2 more years to live.

Dad was right, however, when at age 75, he said seeing the sun rise daily was a little victory.

A popular song starts, "When I am down, and O my soul, how weary..." Yes, some days my soul is weary.

Thank the Lord, I believe that my soul is saved. I do not know how to convince you of such belief, but I am satisfied. Long ago, when I was thirteen, I stood in front of a congregation and said that I believe Jesus the carpenter is the Son of God, and so I believe today. That idea makes me a *bona fide* member of the Christian faith. Such a saying is nonsense to many, and may be to you, but it gives me the Peace of God.

As a result of my faith, and of my age, death is close to me, and I am used to it. The older I get, the less the thought of death bothers me. I also think others would be better off if they went to church in spite of their disbelief.

Yesterday I talked with a patient I'll call Ms. S. She stalled me with a comment, "That talk of death...please stop. I don't want to hear."

Okay, I will try being upbeat with her and tell her of the Three Persons who went into a bar. They were: "Past, Present and Future. The bartender thought they were all Tense."

Ms. S, I found, is not content but is tormented by a pain in her chest. I cannot tell if it is imagined or real; yesterday she was upset about the pain, and moaned that our floor nurse was doing nothing about it. The floor nurse heard, and told me she was quite aware of Ms. S's distress. Constrained by the need to shield the patient's privacy, the nurse later quietly told me that she is waiting for the doctor to call back. So I told Ms. S, and she was able to relax.

Now, if I realize doomsday talk bothers someone, I will instead find cheerful speech. There is an old hymn, "Brighten the corner where you are."

You can brighten your corner of the world by any good deed, and you don't even have to be polite about it. One day, on the Chehalis-Western Trail, I interfered with a couple walking.

"Those two people ahead of you on the trail are holding hands. Can you two do the same?" Because I'm an old geezer, I got away with it. The two laughed and grabbed hands.

Verl Rogers. June 12, 2020. Printed with permission.

Emily's Email

Emily Shaw, age 14

I'm blessed with messages, emails, phone calls, ZOOMS, and facetimes from my loving, teenage grand girls, always keeping me in touch with their latest news from Texas and asking what the latest their Granny and Pawpaw are up to in Panorama Retirement, Lacey, WA.

6-20-2020

Hi Granny!

I'm glad you liked the video! It was something fun to do, and a different experience for this more or less monotonous stay-at-home summer so far. Aside from editing the video, I just finished making a peanut butter bar type thing that has, obviously, peanut butter in it, but also some honey, different types of nuts, and some spices like nutmeg and cinnamon. It's one of my favorite snacks I like to make for the beginning of the school year and in the summer as well.

Every day I look forward to seeing the progress in a bird's nest which is outside my window. About two or three weeks ago, these beautiful black and yellow birds started to make a nest outside my window in a palm tree that's close by. The mother bird started staying in the nest for quite a while each day, so I figured that she'd laid some eggs, and was waiting for them to hatch. One day, I think it was actually this Sunday, she left the nest for a while, and the dad bird started visiting more frequently as well. Recently, I've seen the little chicks stick their little heads out of the nest when one of their parents would return with some food, and I've also seen some of them flapping their little wings! They're so cute!!

What have you been up to lately? Have you been able to do anything around Panorama lately, or is everything still shut down? Have you gotten any favorite foods from the catering service from your restaurant? Hope you're doing well!!!

Love you!
Emily

Laughs and Hugs

Hope Fritchley

Granddaughter Hope: Hope shares love of playing hide and seek with her big Australian Labrador who answers to George. When she hides his toys, he darts around the room and then scoots about the house. His paws make him slither and slide on the hard-floors areas.

Sometimes she hides those rubber toys so hard, he can't find them. Hope gets a big laugh, and George gets a big hug as he grabs it from her hand when, finally, she waves it in front of him.

(Granny Jo's comment): Hope is 13 in 2020, and excels in art, especially people proportions! She is also an excellent golf Junior PGA (Professional Golfers' Association) team member.

Hope Fritchley's 65-pound Labradoodle "George" eagerly awaits his Christmas treat. He remembers that those big red and white "soft socks" always contain special, yummy doggie-treats and a new, exciting toy to entertain himself or to let Hope help him exercise his *obedience* skills.

Billiard Accuracy and Excuses

Verl Rogers

Two or three times a week I play pool with Hershel, Reuben and Neil. All three are better than I, that is, more accurate in hitting the cue ball and bouncing target balls into the pockets of the pool table.

Yet sometimes even the hotshots make mistakes, and some days they do as I do...they miss the pocket more than they hit. And sometimes I win.

Accuracy calls for very close tolerances in making the cue ball; an error as small as $1/32^{nd}$ of an inch at the start of a shot makes a big difference when you are aiming at a target at the far end of the table.

Hershel, when he misses, will ask, "Was I close?" As good friends do, we usually reply, "No, you missed by a mile."

Another good player was Buck Buckman, who died recently. He was a good man; may he rest in peace. Once he told us clearly how the game is played.

"The whole trouble with billiards is accuracy," he said. "The balls are round, and they rebound from the cue ball at a precise 180 degrees from the point they are hit. That is not 179 degrees and 59 minutes, nor 180 degrees and 1 minute: it is 180 degrees *on the dot*!

"You can make excuses if you miss, but no words can make that target ball go into the pocket: the point of impact is controlling. A good player can put a spin on the cue ball, and change the response, but we don't try that often.

"What most of us do is to concentrate. We are all very good at hitting NEARLY, CLOSE, and ALMOST! We do that best."

Even though he's gone, I speak to Buck. "Yes, Buck, I agree. I like to play pool, and my best efforts are like yours: NEARLY, CLOSE, AND ALMOST!"

Verl Rogers. March 6, 2014. Permission to print.

Depression: Home Half Block from the Alamo

Chris Arvid Shaw

After my parents married, they lived in a rooming board house across from the Express Publishing Co., about 5 blocks from the Main Post Office and Alamo Plaza. Charles Robert Shaw was a very thin, lean 6-foot gentleman. He was always polite and gentle. I seldom saw him wear a suit and tie or anything like that. Wilmot (*Grace*) Peterson Shaw was only 5-feet tall, more stocky, very pleasant and helpful.

It was mid-1930s Depression!

After a year or so, my big brother Charles Cornwall Shaw (Charlie) was born. Needing more space for the three of them, Dad began the challenge of looking around in the area, to be close to his job. On his search in the closest downtown neighborhood of Crockett Street were only huge, luxurious homes of the wealthy, except for one: a boarded up, abandoned-for-years old small house at 335 Crockett. Asking around and inquiring, no one seemed to know the owner. Out of desperation, he broke in and set up housekeeping.

After work Dad still continued to search for the owner. I heard he was worried he'd be in trouble and would be fined, have to pay back-charges and possibly be kicked out.

As best as I remember ...

The small 480 square-foot rock and plaster home was German salt-box style...built with a slanted roof so snow could slide off, and not collect, get heavy and cave in. I supposed the immigrants didn't realize that the rare snows ruled: most businesses and all schools closed when it snowed!

Several wooden steps led up to a wooden front porch, which was large in proportion to the rest of the house. Pictures show two 10-foot pillars with ornate woodworking of filigreed designs at the top of each pillar. A banister with lovely curves surrounded the porch, with an opening at the steps.

After a month or so, Ms. Owner began receiving gas and water bills from Public Service. She showed up at "their" door! I'm told she heard my dad's story, his efforts to inquire about the ownership, and his intention to pay back-rent. Observing the meager, sparce necessities, she offered him to pay only $5 a month.

Three years later, Charlie heartily welcomed his little brother, me: Christopher Arvid Shaw. I'm told he always loved me and cared for me, and I experienced that closeness throughout my entire childhood, after he was married, and for the rest of my life, until he died at 86 in 2015.

As you entered the front door, you were in our family bedroom 256 sq. ft. or (16' x 16'), which normally would have been the living room with its fireplace on the right. (We had no access to wood for the fireplace.) The right wall also had a cot (for Charlie) and a double bed for Mother and me. There was one window and a door at the opposite wall on the left.

Stepping another 16 feet into the house, a wall with a center doorway led to the next small room only 8'x 16'. Long curtains on each side of the walkway provided privacy for two renters. Looking back, one area with a bed was for an elderly woman probably in her 60s. The other area across the walk-through was for her adult son, caring for her (and his many beer bottles). They rented 128 square-feet (8' X 16') of our already small home. I don't think they ever used our kitchen. They did have a small, two-burner cooking unit on a table. They paid $5 to us, and we paid that $5 to Ms. Owner for all six of us.

The 12'x8' kitchen with gas stove was detached from the house... the traditional purpose being that if the kitchen caught fire, the rest of the house was not inflamed. The enclosed toilet was at the far end of the kitchen.

With no electricity, we used kerosine lamps. The Zizik Kearns Funeral Home had its garage and shop next door and offered to hook up an electric line to our kitchen. Dad could easily watch that garage area from the side of our house, in case anyone would try to break in.

I remember that Dad slept on a cot in that detached kitchen. In the heat and humidity of the San Antonio summers, he slept outside on that cot at the back of the detached kitchen under the slanted overhang.

Today, the house has been renovated/remodeled. We were disappointed in 2006 when we went to see if it was still standing there. We didn't think it was the same house...not because it was surrounded on three sides by a downtown parking lot. We were looking for the filigreed pillar-tops, and the fancy banister. The "pillars" were simply 4x6 utilitarian supports for the front porch roofing. After peeking through a window, we handed a passerby our camera to get a photo of my wife (Mary Jo), me, and her 91-year-old parents (Winnie and Joe Barbera) posing on the porch.

A Texas historical marker soothed our wounds...somewhat!

Funds for Food and Fun

Chris Arvid Shaw

How do I recall the Great World-Wide Depression of 1929 to 1939 with my older brother Charlie? We lived half a block from the back of the Alamo. All the other homes in the area were much, much larger and much more beautiful than ours. Ours was boarded up, and abandoned for years until Dad broke in for us to have a place for us to live. (That's in another story.)

Mother, was age 34 when I was born in '32; Dad was already 50. She volunteered for the Salvation Army and he eventually worked as a clerk there when he met her. He did different jobs, such as night-watchman for a storage company, and running the Ferris wheel when the carnival came to town for a few weeks. We kids did all kinds of odd jobs to do our little parts to support our family, and also have a dime for the movies and a nickel for popcorn. Brother Charlie was 7, and I was 4.

In the evening when tourists and workers left, we'd climb the walls of the Alamo to play the "battle of the Alamo" games. We were the only ones who escaped!

At times, a neighbor would see us playing outside and ask one of us to rake their leaves. We didn't own a rake, so we used theirs. We liked the extra 25 cents jingling in our pockets. When we noticed lots of leaves in someone's lawn, we'd ask to rake those up, and they'd be glad we asked.

Empty Bottle Routines

Collecting empty soda bottles for return deposit for pennies could be done anywhere, especially around the Alamo area half a block from home. Beer bottles brought in even more pennies.

Our German Catholic neighbors, Mr. and Mrs. Cartridge, owned lots of real estate in San Antonio. Their three-generation family lived across the street from us in a huge 2-story home with a basement. A three-car garage with an apartment was above, for a maid. The Cartridges would invite us to seasonal parties, like Christmas and Halloween. Other times when they'd entertain, or had supper leftovers, they'd send delicious foods to us.

Their daughter and husband lived with them. Mr. Bill Brown was manager of the Crockett Hotel on Bonham St. around the corner from us. The hotel had four tables outside where people left soda bottles. Normally, the janitor collected the bottles, but Mr. Brown let us get them, since he was paying the janitor a nice salary.

Kids Parking Cars?

Mr. Bill Brown's son, Junior Brown, was several years older than we were, and occasionally would organize games or activities for the few neighborhood kids. I remember how he organized a way we could make some money parking cars during the annual Fiesta San Jacinta week. "People are always looking for parking spaces for the several parades next week. You have a place for a car right there on your front lawn, then two cars on the side of the house over there. The Zizik Kearns Funeral Home never uses the entrance/exit on our Crockett Street side. We could get at least four cars by their garage area."

Charlie and I were two excited kids, looking forward to having some spending money. Junior and Charlie printed "Parking 15¢" on three card boards, one for each of us. Then they nailed wooden handles.

L to R: Charlie and brother Chris A. Shaw sell parking space for the Fiesta Parade in San Antonio, TX, in front of their home on 335 Crockett Street behind the Alamo. Junior Brown, from the big house and family across the street, offered the idea to make signs, etc. Notice the *fancy* already parked car!

The big week arrived. Junior demonstrated and said, "Look, hold up your cards so the people can see them, and wave with your other hand to show where to park." We ended up with our pockets full of coins to go to the movies on lots of Saturdays, with popcorn and candy bars.

I have an 8 x 10-inch black and white photo of Charlie and me with our signs during our adventurous day. We didn't own a camera, so I'm sure that Junior Brown had snapped the picture, had it developed and gave it to our family. Until my brother died at age 86 in 2015, we spoke often of how the Cartridge and Brown families shared so generously and cared for our family.

Simple Seining

I remember the path to the Bait Shop with Charlie. Leaving our porch, we turned right on our Crockett Street, walked a half block to Bowie St., turned *left* and walked another half block. There we were! The owner supplied each of us with nets with long handles...like fish-aquarium nets. We each left with a two-gallon bucket with a handle. We weren't going fishing...we were seining for bait minnows in the San Antonio River a few blocks away and down below, about 12 steps. I imitated Charlie, scooping those tiny $1/8^{th}$ to ½ inch little minnows into our nets, and dumping them into the water in our buckets.

When we got tired, or had enough minnows, Mr. Bait Owner would put the smallest ones into his own aquarium to feed until they grew "larger" to a whopping half an inch! None ever grew as long an inch. The big half-inchers were in his other aquarium for fishermen to purchase as fish bait. We probably got a penny for each. Charlie took care of that, since I was only five. Sometimes we didn't sein as many minnows as other days, because there weren't as many in the river. But we'd work until we made about 35 or 40 cents for the day.

Today's News!

We enjoyed selling newspapers every now and then, from the Express Publishing Company which was not quite a mile from our home. Since I was so small, Charlie would take care of the money. We probably brought 40 or 50 cents home.

We sold those newspapers by the Sommers Drug Store on the corner of Broadway and Houston streets, a block away from Alamo Plaza and the Main Post Office. We sold either the Morning Express or the evening Express News several times a week. Charlie was always good, caring, and helpful to me. If I needed change for the customer, he'd put the proper coins in my opened 4-year-old hand. We got a penny for each copy we sold.

I especially remember a couple of Mexican men who kindly asked us to leave the space in front of Sommers Drug at Broadway and Houston. We had seen them selling papers there a long time. It was their spot, and they had to feed their families. They probably figured we were just making extra spending money to go to the movies. We gladly moved across the street by the Zales Jewelry Store.

Selling the papers was fun, but in the summertime, we went barefooted. Too hot in the 90+ degrees and 95-degree humidity in San Antonio. But standing in the same place on the blazing concrete for hours, our feet got really hot.

Then there was the time a man came and bought one of my papers and handed me 50 cents! I went over to Charlie to get change and when I turned around, the man was already walking away. I ran to catch up. He was already about a half block away down Broadway. I was calling "Mister, Mister…" Huffing and puffing, I held out my hand. "Mister, here is your change."

He said to me. "I don't need any change." He turned and walked inside the Travelers' Hotel.

I went back to tell Charlie, "The man said he didn't need any change."

Charlie burst out, "WOW!"

I figured *that must be lots of money*!

The Art of Compromise

Bob Bower

From personal experience I can say, when you love parenting your first child and decide to have a second child—someone must compromise if the whole gaggle is going to survive! I remember vividly when our little girl was born. She was a lovely little black-haired girl. She joined her 32 pound two-year-old brother in our nursery. He woke up every morning at 5:30 a.m. I fed him his breakfast and put him in his playpen to play with his toys while I was doing some early morning reading. His mother and I had compromised to allow her to sleep later each day. He went to bed promptly in the evening at 6 p.m. and never made a peep until 5:30 the next morning.

Our newest child, Carolyn, slept soundly until just about noon. That was because she had spent from 6 p.m. until midnight the evening before fussing and crying with what all of us parents and grandparents used to call "the colic." We even put our children in the car and went for a short drive to calm our precious tiny one, only to find that she was prone to motion sickness. My wife and I took turns at moving the jiggling baby-buggy back and forth from the spot where we were lying in bed—thinking we were lulling her to sleep. Our consistent rocking only lulled us to sleep. Then she woke us up with her even more fervent crying. No one compromised. It was a fight to the draw. I still love her. As I write in July 2019, she turns 56 in October. Eleven days later her brother turns 58. They both have gray hair now. What little I have is white and I sleep soundly most nights!

Twenty-five years of education from kindergarten through two master's degrees taught me a lot about compromise. Marriage to a woman I loved, and who loved me, taught both of us that the art of compromise makes each of us better and enriches life beyond imagination.

Gene and Me: Frankenstein

Tom Allen

When darkness fell, I put on ski boots, football shoulder pads, an oversized coat, and Gene's Frankenstein mask. That mask was padded inside to bring me to seven feet tall. Then we would go to the Drive-in Root Beer stand to order food from the roller-skating car hops. I couldn't talk too well, so Gene would order while the girl watched outside the car window. The first girl sent another with the tray of food, and still another followed to see the backseat passenger. Their expressions were priceless.

At night Frankenstein should be found in a cemetery, so we took our dates along with Frankenstein. When a car appeared around the corner, a girl could be seen running across the street chased by a monster. Most cars sped up and quickly left. One stopped and asked Gene's date if she needed help. She calmly said no, she just lived over there, and she went among the tombstones.

That same girl, Gene's date, joined us at Gene's house for a party. We were playing charades. Gene's date was performing a charade. Behind her at the picture window, I saw another Frankenstein appear. Gene's little brother had the same type of humor as his brother! So I tried to signal Gene across the room. He didn't get the signal, but his date did. She turned, saw Frankenstein, and passed out flat on the floor.

That did it! They were married later that year.
Who needed television?!

Finding Easter Ride

Mary Jo Shaw

Kids look for Easter eggs. I looked for an Easter *ride*.

Living at Panorama Retirement and Convalescent Center in Lacey, Washington, I called Elaine, my neighbor to remind her.

"I'll be delighted take you in the morning to Mass. I love that you go with me," she said. But a few hours later, she ended up in the hospital emergency room with very high blood pressure and horrible headache. She sent word she wouldn't be taking me the next morning, Easter Sunday.

I called Sally, a resident who often attends on Sunday mornings. Fine! She'd pick me up 45 minutes earlier so we could get a good parking space and a seat, since Sacred Heart Church would be very crowded for the annual celebration.

Easter: a car drives up. I didn't recall Sally's car description, but I ran out and opened the passenger door. I recognized the resident's face, and hadn't seen Sally in a long time, so I asked, "Oh, are you Sally?"

"No, I'm Rosemary. I'm taking you to church."

Still standing outside, I asked, "What happened to Sally?"

"Who's Sally?"

"I called *her* to take me to Mass." I stared at her. "Are you a Catholic?"

"Yes," she said smiling with her hands on the steering wheel. "I usually go to St. Columbine's on the edge of town."

I knew her name and recognized her face as a Panorama resident. I'd signed her up for events at the activity desk, but I'd forgotten the face that matched the name.

Time was ticking, so I hopped in and shut the door. We chuckled at the situation as she drove.

I turned toward her, "Did you change your Easter plans to *volunteer taking me* to church?" I was amazed at her generosity.

"That's okay," she said. "Sacred Heart Church is closer anyway. What number did you dial?"

"I don't know! Obviously, it was wrong. **You** know it—I dialed **your** number!"

We laughed until our stomachs ached and wondered about the odds of dialing a wrong number, getting a Catholic person who was also a Panorama resident, and one who was willing to take me to church.

During the ceremony, I strove to avoid seeing her jittering shoulders, as she peered side-glances at me, also struggling to retain from giggling. This through the entire, extra-long Easter service!

After Mass, both of us breathed exhaustion from the strain and sat in our pew until the congregation exited. Rosemary uncontrollably exploded, **"Mary Jo, you need to buy a lottery ticket. You'd have better odds at winning the lottery than anyone else!"** Our laughing outburst flared up worse, especially, when I looked at the altar with a sincere, audible request, "Please, Lord, we really have done our best to be reverent."

Pondering a few seconds, I whispered, "Rosemary, I believe God is working here." She smiled and nodded.

This was in 2015. Still today, when we meet on our campus, our memorable coincidence triggers our laughter.

I had a blessed celebration, and found the best Easter egg that year. It's in the shape of a bighearted friend at our Panorama Retirement. Amen!

A French Kiss

Sally Vogel, author of 24 books on Blurb

It was an early summer day in the Southern Sierra and I had found a rough granite boulder to perch upon. I love getting away from the noise of civilization and this place suited me fine. I surveyed my surroundings from my hillside perch and listened to the "ker ker" of a pair of ravens keeping in touch while flying about in search of food, and to the long rambling melodies of a California thrasher backed by various chirps and tweets from smaller birds flitting about in the shrubs. From far below, the rushings and rumblings of the Kern River joined this mountain song.

I was wearing my stylish new bargain sun glasses. Their reflective orange coating hid my eyes from the world but allowed me to see out just fine. It didn't surprise me too much when a juvenile hummingbird approached, came within 2 inches of my glasses, and hovered for a few seconds. I sat very still, not wanting the bird to discover that there was a person there. It puzzled over the orange reflection and then flew off. But wait! A few seconds later it came back and once again hovered in front of my face. This was no passive second take. Mistaking my mouth for a flower, it inserted its slender cool tongue between my lips. Wow! I was elated to have been mistaken for a flower!

Il Volo - Musicians par Excellence

Martha Trupp

At some point, through PBS or Amazon, I discovered Il Volo ("The Flight"), an Italian group of two tenors and a baritone singing operatic pop, or opera with a modern touch. As young boys, they each participated in festivals and competitions and won many of them. At a 2009 talent show, at which they each participated when they were around 15, an idea was formulated to bring the three voices together. The rest is history for them and their families.

It was after I saw them in San Jose, CA, in 2016 that I became more curious. When I returned home, I started researching. Here is a bit of my study:

> Piero Barone grew up in Sicily and is the son of a mechanic and a homemaker. His maternal grandfather, a blind musician, recognized Piero's voice when Piero was a toddler and paid for his piano lessons. Piero sang at weddings to pay for his own singing lessons, and spent his teenage years traveling with Il Volo. It is said he has his grandfather's voice. He can hold notes for extended periods, and goes higher than expected. His voice is rich and gravely—one of a kind.
>
> Ignazio Boschetto also grew up in Sicily. He is a lyric tenor who, at age three, sang arias in his bedroom, shocking his mother when she checked in on him. He plays piano, guitar, and drums, composes and arranges music, and owns a production company. He helps out in his family's pizza parlor on occasion.

He's the most comical and exuberant of the three on stage, but he has a powerful voice that can fill the farthest reaches of an auditorium with his emotional renditions.

His range is wide; his high notes pure and clear with lighter tones.

Gianluca Ginoble was exposed to a wide range of music early in life and like the others, began singing around age three. He's the baritone, and often starts the songs that the threesome sings. He has a seductive and mellow voice, and his execution is flawless. His early shyness comes through at times, and he is studying piano. Gianluca lives near his family in Montepagano, a small village in the Abruzzo region of Italy.

Piero, Ignazio, and Gianluca all have gained a facility for languages. Gianluca speaks English like we do. They sing in Spanish, German, Italian, English, French, and Latin, and are learning Portuguese.

All three are from modest, humble Catholic backgrounds, and got their start singing in church. Since meeting in 2009, they consider each other as brothers. During the Coronavirus, they secluded themselves.

In 2017 in Mexico City, where I saw them for the second time, the audience went wild. Young women screamed and rushed the stage. I had a Meet & Greet ticket to see them and after standing in line for more than an hour, I entered the room with great anticipation, but was shocked when someone urgently pulled on my arm and tried to convince me to leave. I reacted somewhat stubbornly, but—there was an earthquake. We went to an area in between tall buildings, where I wondered about our safety, but where the remaining Meet and Greet was set up. There was no time to talk but I got my hugs and a photo with them, which I'm treasuring the rest of my life. I've seen Il Volo twice since then, in Monaco in 2018, and San Jose, CA, in 2020.

Il Volo is well-known and popular in Italy, and sing for tens of thousands. Piero, Ignazio, and Gianluca contribute to their families, their communities, and to their country and are celebrated wherever they go. When I traveled in Italy in 2018, it was a delight when the tour guide indulged my request for Il Volo music during the hours-long bus drive through the countryside.

Through their performances, Il Volo expresses in every way the tenet they espouse, that they are "Three Voices: One Soul." Loved by women and men, they appeal to all ages. I appreciate young talent and find their story especially interesting. They bring Italian culture to the world. They unite. They are musicians par excellence.

Paid In Full

Lois Williams

"And by that will, we have been made holy through the sacrifice of the body of Jesus Christ once for all, because by one sacrifice he has made perfect forever those who are being made holy." Hebrews 10:10, 12 (NIV)

Writing checks to pay the bills
the other day I was musing,
wondering how it would be if I
didn't have to pay any bills;
if everything was paid for and
there would be no more little
window envelopes filling the mailbox.

Something I had read recently
about managing debt came to mind,
advice given to struggling individuals:
Refinance, consolidate,
borrow creatively and,
failing all else, seek help.
But none of these takes away the debt
it only changes the creditor.

My thoughts turned to
the debt of sin we owe.
Man tries all sorts of ways to bargain,

to brush away the phantom,
yet the debt never goes away
until all else fails and he seeks help,
and Discovers, that,
should we choose to accept it,
the Master in Charge has given us
a Visa for heaven, paid in full!

Reprinted by permission, from "Psalms From The Pathway",
Xulon Press © 2003 by Lois Williams
Email: fredlowill@msn.com

Beginning to Teach at 100

Mary Jo Shaw

It embarrassingly happened in August of 1960, on my first mission as a nun in Abilene, TX.

I was eager, but nervous as I sat balancing on a stool pulled out from the small telephone table in the Sisters' community room. I gripped a list of music students that last year's teacher had left in the studio for herself or for the new music teacher who might be assigned there...*me!* Just voice, no visual contact...yet!

I was teaching 11-year-old Jerry S. a clarinet lesson. In the middle of playing, he stopped, but kept his instrument close to his mouth to ask, "Sister, my dad thinks you're 18. How old *are* you?"

Not wanting him to know I had just turned 21, and only 2 or 3 years older than our husky football players, I teased, "Oh, I'm going on 100."

He immediately continued his clarinet playing.

The next week or so, Mr. and Mrs. S arrived at the Meet the Teacher Open House and sheepishly stepped into my small studio. "Is Sister Mary Janet available?"

"Yes, *I'm* Sister Mary Janet."

Their eyes bulged. "Oh, you *are* young. Our son, Jerry..."

This poor couple needed help!

Immediately I laughed, "Oh, we *veteran* Sisters are used to all kinds of out-of-the-mouths-of-babes' incidents. Don't worry about it. Someday someone should put them in a book."

So...I just did!

God's Plan to Meet for Patti

Patti Lynch

You remember I (author, Mary Jo Shaw) am the oldest of six girls. I share this inspiring long-distance phone conversation with my sister Patti Lynch (number 3 in our sibling line-up):

"After I moved here," Patti said, "we got a new pastor. Joe Jr (Patti's son) and wife Heather, and I went to their friend's home for a small gathering. We were to meet the new pastor who asked us to introduce ourselves and tell a little about ourselves. We each spoke out loud to the group. I told how I was Joe's mom and had just moved to Ohio from Texas."

Patti sounded excited, but I interrupted, "Hey, Patti, slow down so I could take some notes to tell Chris!"

She continued at slower pace, but kept her enthusiasm. "After everyone had spoken, Linda came across the room right up to me. She introduced herself and said she would like my phone number. My eyes bulged! I wondered why."

In her sweet voice Linda said, "Patti, I'd really like to get together and so I can get to *know* you better."

"I was thrilled!! I didn't have any of my own friends yet. Only two days later she called and asked if I'd join her and a friend to go to the movies!"

I put my pencil down to stretch my fingers. "What a story, Patti! Tell me more about this Linda!"

"Mary Jo, would you believe...Linda has 11 siblings! She lives about 10 miles from me, and we go to the same church!

"This past Christmas Joe and Heather were out of town. Linda and her husband invited me for Christmas dinner. One of their daughters and her husband were there, also one of Linda's sisters from California. I felt so at home with all of them. It was a blast!

"We have been best of friends since. I really love her. I know it was God who put us together that night...when we met the new pastor."

(Thank you for sharing your story, Patti!)

Mad-Lib Miranda

Bill Clow

We used to live next door to a school. It was very convenient for our son and his wife to bring Miranda, our amazing granddaughter, to us in the morning, so that she could go to school during the day. Then we did homework with her until her parents come to pick her up after work.

This story involves a flash of insight. You know, that burst of comprehension that lights a person up when he or she comes to understand something.

Miranda and I worked for months on three words: **noun, verb** and **adjective**. We had many conversations like the following:

"Miranda, consider this sentence: *I like easy homework*. What is *like*?"

"*Like* is an adjective."

"Actually, *like* is a verb. What is *easy*?"

"*Easy* is a noun."

"No, *easy* is an adjective. What is *homework*?"

"*Homework* is a verb."

"No, *homework* is a noun."

Now, we have to jump to the weekend. Miranda and my wife and I often go camping in our RV. On this weekend we drove to Soap Lake in Eastern Washington and set up our camp. Afterwards, Miranda and I went for a swim until some obnoxious boys came along and, just by their boisterous behavior, took over the pool for themselves. Miranda and I came back to camp and sat down at the picnic table.

I pulled out a book of Mad-Libs.

"Miranda, give me a verb."

"*Smell.*"

"Give me an adjective."

"*Stinky.*"

"Give me a noun."

"*Boys.*"

"Now, listen to this," I said. "I smell stinky boys."

We both laughed at our own great wit.

"This isn't like homework," Miranda said. "It's too much fun."

Then Miranda exploded with inner insight. She caught her breath and her eyes lit up. I could tell that finally, she understood nouns, verbs and adjectives.

"Grandpa," she said. Give me a verb."

"*Love.*"

"Give me an adjective."

"*Smart.*"

"Give me a noun."

"*Grandpa.*"

"Listen to this! I love a smart grandpa."

For two more days in camp and while driving home in the RV, we did Mad-Libs non-stop.

Baby Baths

Verl Rogers

It has been 57 years since our first baby, Susan, was born and 55 years since our second child, Nancy, was born, but a favorite memory of mine is their baths when they were small. At first Janet washed them in the kitchen sink.

She must have started the baby baths very soon after we brought them home from the hospital, but I was at work and did not see a bath until a weekend. In the meantime I had a strange delusion that it was Janet who was naked in the kitchen sink. She didn't fit. Finally one Saturday I got to watch.

Janet kept up a steady chatter for each bath. "You are going to like this warm water and the soap and the splashing, and I will wash you all over, and your hair, and your feet and toes and hands and fingers and that little nose and chin and your belly and your back and your bottom and legs and just everything!" By the time the chatter was finished, the soaping was done and the rinsing had begun.

I asked, "What if she gets soap in her eyes?"

"Oh, look at the label on the bottle 'Guaranteed safe for the eyes.'"

Soaps have changed greatly since our girls were small. It may have been a Castile soap from Johnson Wax that Janet used then, or it may have been Dr. Bronner's. Whichever it was, it was safe for babies. They never cried when soapy water ran down into their eyes.

When Janet first said she bathed the baby in the sink, I had my doubts, but it worked out very well. We had a little plastic tub, baby size, and Janet carefully kept the faucet away from the baby's head.

The kitchen counter was just the right height to lay out a towel and pat the little body dry.

When the little girl grew too big, Janet just moved to the tub in the bathroom.

The babies loved the bath. They would gurgle and wave arms and legs madly. There was always plenty of splashing.

My memory is vague on Nancy's age, our second child, when Janet put both into the bathtub at once, but I have a clear memory of the two together. It was always loads of fun, the two in the tub. There was laughing and giggling, never a quiet moment.

Now in 2013, I am 86 years old. I have a great-grand-daughter two years old, Caleigh. She cheers me greatly along with Nancy and other family members. And I always smile when I remember either baby in the kitchen sink.

Verl Rogers. Used with permission

Romantic Night in Florence

Don Ulrich

In August of 1966, Carol and I had been married two years when we packed Erick Frommer's book *Europe on 5 Dollars a Day* and headed to London, France, Rome, etc. and back to London. We had two more weeks of sightseeing yet to go!

While in Florence we stayed in a fourth-class pensione. This was a small private home with a bath we shared with the owner. Nowadays, we might call this a B&B.

After our first full day of seeing the sights, we returned to the pensione after the sun had been asleep several hours. Our house key to the front door was so huge and heavy, I had to wear a sport coat with a big pocket for the key to fit. It was about 9 inches long and ½ inch in diameter. Honest!

No wonder that key was so big…it had to open a heavy huge door that was 10 feet high and about 4 inches thick.

On entering the house, all was quiet. We tiptoed down the hall to our bedroom and were puzzled with what we saw. The room was lit with four or five votive candles. (**Votive candles** are in an area in Catholic churches lined up in several rows to be lit with a provided long wick, lit from a neighboring candle. The person who lit the candle makes monetary donation, kneel, and prays for his/her special intention.)

After studying the pleasant sight of the candles, we took a few steps to our bed. The bed cover was neatly pulled down. And the bedsheets were sprinkled with red rose petals. The aroma was absolutely delightful.

So romantic!

Carol shook her head, grinned and whispered, "Don, the owner actually questioned me this morning. She asked, 'Carol, you mean you've been married two years and you don't have any babies yet? She even asked whether I was pregnant yet!'"

"No," Carol answered to both questions.

I replied, "That's really strange. Never heard of such quizzing." Pausing to think, I shrugged my shoulders. "Oh well, we *do* get to enjoy a romantic evening, and have an amusing story to take home to Cincinnati, Ohio!"

BY THE WAY: the next year, we had our first precious baby, Bryce. Then three years later in 1970, we welcomed Brittany. In 1973, we had another **B**...Brandon.

And this *was* great...a story to bring home...and to point to in this book!

Melpomene and Me

Bill Clow

Melpomene: Oh, there you are!

Me: I was only gone for a minute! I just went to get the mail.

Melpomene: I thought you were going to work.

Me: No way! I'm retired. I haven't gone to work for at least five years.

Melpomene: How about those vacations, then? You left me all by myself for weeks!

Me: We never left you for more than a week. Besides, you had plenty of food, water and litter.

Melpomene: It seemed like forever.

Me: Well now I can't go anywhere. We're stuck with each other. Let me pet you.

Melpomene: I need a cat treat! Please give me a cat treat!

Me: Okay! Okay! Here!

Melpomene: Thank you.

Me: And people think that cats don't say thank you!

Melpomene: Master, would you sit down please?

Me: Okay! How's this? Aah! I'm in my favorite easy chair.

Melpomene: I'm going to jump up and sit in your lap.

Me: Please do. You have the loudest purr!

Melpomene: It's because I love you, master.

Me: Thank you, Melpomene. I love you too. How could we get along without each other?

Melpomene: I don't know, master. Thank God we have each other to talk to.

Elizabeth and Israel, 1778

Ernesta Ballard

In 1777 the Revolutionary War was underway. Philadelphia was in the sights of the British army which had recently occupied New York. The Continental Congress would soon leave the city for safety in Lancaster, 40 miles away. George Washington was moving his army into winter quarters at Valley Forge. Philadelphia had been founded by Quakers, and the Philadelphia Quaker meeting included many men prominent in business, politics and civic life.

The Quakers had taken a firm stance against armed insurrection. They were pacifists, not loyalists. They agreed with the grievances that led to separation, but not the method. Their fellow citizens and community leaders distrusted the Quakers and increasingly harassed them for their views.

Among the most outspoken Quakers was Henry Drinker. As their position became increasingly untenable, he and several other men were arrested. They were sentenced to prison and sent 200 miles south to Winchester, Virginia. There they were made comfortable but confined. Months went by. The prisoners' wives remained in Philadelphia where they took over the management of family, businesses and community affairs. The war enveloped them when the British occupied the city.

By spring the British had moved out and four of the wives determined to travel to the Congress in Lancaster with a petition to free their husbands. To make this journey they would first have to go to Valley Forge to get a pass from George Washington which would allow them to make the trip. As they made their preparations, members of the Quaker meeting feared for their safety and urged the four women to take along a man. The women assented on the condition that whoever was chosen agree to be an escort for safety and not a spokesman for their cause. They intended to present their own case and would not accept a subordinate role.

When all was agreed and a suitable escort identified, the party set off. They were successful in all. General Washington provided the necessary pass and Congress the pardon. One of the four women was Elizabeth Drinker. She and her husband Henry were my great, great, great, great grandparents. (Counting my grandparents, my parents and me we are separated by seven generations) The escort who cooperated with the women in their expedition and proceeded as they had planned was Israel Morris. My friend and neighbor here at Panorama, Dave Morris, is a direct descendant of Israel's. Imagine. A shared legacy.

Gene and Me: Tricky Dick

Tom Allen

Dick was older than Gene and me. The only time he didn't know everything was the day he did a jig behind the school. We were just listenin' when all of sudden he starts jumping around slapping at his right leg and yelling, "Yow, Yow, Yow!" Gene and I didn't know what to make of it all. Then he stops, shakes his leg, and a dead little mouse rolls out on to the ground. We'd never seen a mouse run up anybody's leg before.

Dick always did things different anyway. I remember the day he showed us how to high jump. Gene and I dug a hole in a vacant lot next to his house. We filled it with sand, put two sticks on either side with nails in it. A fishin' pole served as our high jump bar. We could jump pretty high, considerin' the nail height. However, the center was most popular because it sagged at least six inches. Gene jumped from the left and me from the right.

Dick watched a while sizing up the situation. "You guys are doing it all wrong. I'll show you the right way," he says.

"We are doin' it the right way. Everybody does it our way." We had read all about high jumping and knew we were right.

"No, no, the best way is to jump head first over the bar," claims Dick.

"But that's illegal."

"I don't care, it's the best way. I'll show you."

"You better not, you might get hurt."

"Not me, watch this." Then away Dick goes, straight at the bar. Up over, head first, he flies and "whump" into the sand. It was remarkable. There he was...balancing on his face...legs and body straight up. He teetered back and forth about a foot, still balanced on his face!

Gene looked at me, and we both rushed up to the high jump pit. Dick wasn't making a sound. He just remained in that remarkable position!

We pushed his legs down and his face came out of the sand. He slowly got up without looking at us and walked away!

Gene and I decided then and there to keep doin' it the legal way!

Writing Prompt Signs

Mary Lee

Going to the Camden Writer's Workshop Saturday morning, I saw an American flag and cannon. I pointed to them and said, "On the way home, let's take a picture of this for my Wednesday writing class."

Chuck said, "Interesting writers' prompt."

Time passed quickly at the workshop. Returning home, the flag and cannon were harder to spot. We missed it.

We turned around in the driveway of a run-down building, in the picture that I chose *not* to write about.

Getting back to the flag and cannon, we see that it is on private property with "No Trespassing".

Preferring not to be shot or attacked by dogs, I said, "Go back. Take a picture of that ugly blue and white, forgotten building."

Chuck said, "Not much to look at but it has a parking lot with access to get the picture."

With all this back and forth, I'm not sure exactly where I spotted this sign, in the picture I *did* choose to write about.

I do better with word prompts than with picture prompts so this turn of events was welcome.

Thinking about the words on the sign *Taste of Heaven Art Studio*, I wondered, "What would Heaven taste like?" I thought of three "tastes" that I would want Heaven to taste like.

Birthday cake ice cream, so sweet it tastes like birthday cake *icing*, but no dry cake underneath only refreshing ice cream.

Next taste of Heaven would be my husband's chocolate cobbler.

The chocolate filling is made with cocoa, best tasting chocolate ever; silky smooth, ah heavenly.

The last taste would be pizza, piled high with Italian sausage, mushrooms, and onions, layered on a slightly crisp crust hot from the oven.

Mary Lee, Author of 5 Children's Books,
including *When Grandma's False Teeth Fly*

Music Prayer's Long-Lasting Journey

Mary Jo Shaw

In the treasured years of formation in a convent for 13 years, I looked forward to our group's wheeling the retired nuns to our postulate study-room to play cards or games. It was a win-win, although very elderly Sister Helen left happy, *only* if she had won! I loved volunteering to play with her and escorting her back to her room to hear… through her loose dentures: "I have a 100% track-record of winning… every time I come!"

I'd smile. "O-h-h, ye-s-s, Sister Helen!"

Getting along well with the aged, I loved hearing stories of before and after they were nuns. I have visited the convent many times after leaving and still communicate and receive their quarterly newsletters.

My fondest dream had been to share my music with residents in retirement homes.

During my 55 years of teaching, we prayed before each student's piano lesson, "Every note we sing and pray, will be for You, O Lord, today." After I was married, I had many talented students of all ages coming to our home before and/or after school, even on Saturday mornings.

Was it permissible to call the retirement homes, asking to allow my students to entertain? Would the parents be available and willing to bring the children at the appropriate day and time? I stormed heaven for an answer.

What? What was I thinking? Since childhood, I've always depended on God to help me in my challenges, and He always came through, *if* it was His will. Thus, I again prayed very sincerely, and fervently that *if* God wanted me to gather my piano students, He'd come up with a way...after all He IS God!

You've probably heard that we are to *work* as if it all depended on us, but to *pray* as if it all depended on God. Monday, I finished writing a few more notations to mention during my planned call. I was waiting for a piano student to show up any minute, when...DING-DONG-DING-DONG.

Wendy, a musician herself, showed up with her teenager Elise. Wendy asked, "Mary Jo, we just moved my mother into that nice new retirement center about a mile away from you. The activity director is looking for entertainers of all kinds. We love your recitals...your students always play well, and selections are fun, with lots of variety for everyone. Would you consider having your students perform about a half hour?"

My jaw dropped. I shared how I had just finished my prayer, and showed her my tablet with final notes for my phone call.

"Sounds like an answer to your prayer!" Wendy and Elise said in unison. "I won't say anything to the director, Mary Jo. I'll just let you take it from here."

Needless to say, Ms. Director (I'll call Cindy) nearly came through the phone! "You are an answer to my prayers, Mary Jo! I'm newly certified, and this is my first job. I'm *so* excited at this! I prayed with my husband last night that God would help me find people interested. We just opened up, so all of us are new, even the residents. I'm a firm believer in asking God's help. He has never let me down. But this is better than I expected."

Then the fragile question, "Mary Jo, how many students will be playing? How much is the charge?"

I revealed *my* story of how I prayed to have my class accepted by a retirement center. "I'd like the children to realize how much joy they give others simply by volunteering their God-given talents. That's plenty pay!"

The event? Informal. No printed programs handed out. I would call each student to the piano and announce the composition. (I had 55 years of recitals to practice projecting my voice!)

Remember: all residents at Cindy's retirement were new. The day we showed up, movers and residents' family members were also showing up. The entire structure, inside and out, was marbleized, steps, porch, pillars, flooring. Just inside, we passed an open office, elevator, a staircase, and crossed the hallway into a formal visiting area of plush wing-backed chairs. The room showcased a shiny grand piano at one end. One resident moving in that very day, insisted, "I taught piano all my life. I'm not missing those kids for anything." She initiated a welcomed, Q/A session at the end of our program!

(Many local music teachers were thrilled with the idea as a summer involvement.)

No two events were alike. I prepared the students to interact, down physically to the level of the resident. "Observe whether they have a hard time hearing. Thank them for coming to listen. Ask *residents* questions. Where did they grow up? Hobbies? What was different when you were in school? Did you play any musical instruments?"

That was then. This is now:

In 2011, hubby Chris and I retired and moved to Panorama Retirement in Lacey, WA. Would you believe? I never realized my major volunteer service here would be entertaining with background piano music for resident activities. These include monthly birthday dinners, or in our Convalescent/Rehabilitation Center, and weekly lunch times in assisted living, campus chapel services, etc. Residents come to the piano and whisper, "Mary Jo, we just love your variety of pieces...classics, old-time favorites, rags, hymns, waltzes, and the *way* you play. Thank you so much!"

How can I ever thank my Heavenly Father for answering my sincere prayers all of my life! The more I simply make others happy by *sharing* the gift of music He has given to me, the more *joy I receive* from Him. I pray to be able to bear all that my God sends. Truly I am blessed...over and above.

Cotton Candy Up-tic, Miranda?

Bill Clow

I am a baseball fan. My grand-daughter Miranda is a cotton candy fan. I don't have to tell you that baseball and cotton candy go together and you won't be surprised, then, when I tell you that Miranda and I have attended several Seattle Mariner baseball games.

One day, as we were watching a game, after I had allowed Miranda to have three vitamin-enriched, organic cotton candies, the Mariners were trailing three to nothing as they came to bat in the bottom of the ninth inning. The first Mariner came to the plate.

"Grandpa," said Miranda, "can I have one more cotton candy?"

"No, Miranda. The game will be over in a few minutes."

"What if he gets on base?"

"Then you can have a cotton candy. But remember—Grandma says you can't eat cotton candy in the car!"

"Ball one," said Miranda.

"Whoa! You can't call the balls and strikes before he's even pitched them!"

Miranda rolled her eyes at me.

The first pitch came. Low and outside. One and oh.

"Ball two," predicted Miranda.

The second pitch was in the dirt. Two and oh.

"Ball three," said Miranda.

The pitch was high and wild. Three and oh.

"Ball four," said Miranda.

The pitch was again in the dirt. The batter undid his shin guards and trotted down to first base.

"Okay, Grandpa. Can I have some money?"

Stern grand-father that I am, I gave her a five-dollar bill and she skippity-hopped over to the nearest cotton candy vendor.

The next batter grounded out to second base. So did the next one. Two out. The game would be over in a minute. (I had a *vision* of Grandma getting into the passenger seat and asking, "Why is everything so sticky?")

Miranda came back, pinching off pink wads and stuffing them into her mouth. "Ball one," she said as she took her seat.

"Oh, you think you can predict the pitches again!"

Ball one crossed low across the plate. With sudden shock, I realized what Miranda was doing. I couldn't believe it!

"Ball two," called Miranda.

Ball two almost hit the batter.

"How do you do that?" I asked.

"I just concentrate and somehow it happens," said Miranda. "Watch! —Ball three."

The pitch was wide. Ball three.

"Are you a witch?" I asked.

"Hardly. I only wish good things for good people—like the Mariners."

She looked at me and then back at the batter. "Ball four," she said.

Ball four was low and outside.

"Hey, you've got two men on! If the next guy walks, the bases are loaded."

He walked, just as Miranda called it. Bases loaded. Bottom of the ninth. Three to nothing in favor of the Yankees.

Miranda looked at me and smiled. Slowly and deliberately, she pronounced "Home run!" She smiled and winked at me and then turned her attention back to the game.

    I don't have to tell you what happened next. I will tell you though that, right after the game, I bought season tickets for the two of us.

    And, oh yes—there was an unexplainable up-tick that year in the sales of cotton candy.

My Roast For My Brother's 50th Birthday Party

Sally Vogel, author, 24 books on Blurb

Once upon a time.....a long, long, LONG time ago, little Dickie was born. Brother to a princess. Now Dickie wasn't a prince, because we all know what Dickies grow up to be. However, his sister, the princess, didn't know this and she played with her little brother for as long as he was smaller than she was.

Time passed, and one day, when the princess came home from school, she saw a FIRE TRUCK and a POLICEMAN at her house. What could have happened? Oh, no! Look, look, see Dickie getting in trouble with the police. Little Dickie had begun an early investigation into career opportunities. Fortunately, his foray into arson was nipped in the bud and it was only the vacant lot that burned and not the houses next to it.

Dickie had a wonderful toy. It was called a Flexie Flyer. His second career investigation was into that of an adventurer. Belly down on this wonderful vehicle, Dickie explored the tunnels beneath the city. Daring black widows, old balloons, cockroaches and who knows what other horrors, he traversed the neighborhood, unseen by the rest of the world. This, too, was a dead-end career.

But in high school, Dickie, now grown into a Dick, tried another career. This career shall go unmentioned here, but fortunately, it too was nipped in the bud and Dick was sent far away to repent and to further his education in a more structured setting.

Once again, Dick had ideas other than those of his parents, and decided his education would take a different direction. Forget the books! Forget going to class! He explored another career. He decided to recapture some of that adventure he found flying through the tunnels by flying through the air! He would become a pilot. He did.

Poor mother and father. What to do. But by this time it was too late to do anything. It was up to Dick.

So Dick, now deciding it was maybe better to be a Richard, got married to the girl back home, had 3 kids and got responsible. He joined the Air Force. He got a high school diploma. He became.... successful.

Electric Shock

Verl Rogers

My niece Beth works at Puget Power (PSE), where she supervises outside contractors, mostly in cutting tree branches that threaten power lines. Every storm brings outages, and Beth then calls her stable of contractors, a few out-of-state, to repair downed lines. Puget has a long-term program to bury power lines, but many areas remain where the wires are on poles, vulnerable to falling trees and icing.

There is a muddle of street lights, some owned by Puget, others owned by municipalities and a few private companies, that Beth also supervises. She tries to renew street lights on a four-or-five-year rotation. However, in a storm, she gets every repair done quickly.

The Puget poles also carry telephone and TV cables, where the other utility rents space, often at $10 per pole per year. Here is where she had a severe emergency last year.

There was a bad storm and one intersection had a light torn out as well as two or three poles carrying a 12,000-volt power line and a few TV cables. Beth dispatched an outside crew to the corner, where they found two main wires on the ground. They stretched yellow tape to fence off the danger, but a worker from Wave Communications tried to enter and work on his TV cable.

The Puget contractor's men warned the Wave man, but he was under pressure to get the job done, persisted and touched a 12,000-volt line, then fell on it. A contractor grabbed an insulated pole to push the victim off the hot wire, but got a shock himself. Both men were taken to the hospital. The Wave man lost an arm, and pieces of his flesh and clothing were scattered around. The savior was burned a few places, but recovered in a few days.

Beth said, "The contractor saved the man's life, but he was still shaken when I met him a few days later. In fact, the whole crew was emotional."

The victim recovered, but only after 45 days in the hospital.

Beth said, "The situation was so serious that I visited both victim and savior several times. It surprised me that the two became friends, and they had a family barbecue last month."

"Beth," I commented, "that is good policy, to keep up with your crews."

"Oh, we get all tangled up together—over the years we work together many times. I feel it is not only good business, but good personally, to visit the crews. After a big storm, we have to know one another, or we never get the work done."

"Do you have legal problems with right-of-way owners?"

Beth replied, "Very seldom. Today I met with a PSE person and your Panorama Retirement manager to discuss many things, including trimming some trees over on Golf Club Road. That is an insulated line, but still the insulation can be cooked if a tree branch rubs for a time. We had a good conversation and both sides are satisfied now."

Beth makes me proud to be her uncle.

Verl Rogers. May 31, 2016. Permission to print.

Warning: No Baby Bends!

May St. Peter

May, pregnant with her second child, was bending over, lugging wet laundry from the open door on the side of the washing machine. Her four-year old watched with wide eyes, "Oh, Mommie, don't bend over. You might bend the baby!"

The Bakery

Chuck Lyon

Bill Story, my classmate and relatively close neighbor, somehow got a job in the local bakery in Lake City, WA. It wasn't a very inspiring occupation in 1937, but this was during the time when there was a strong public clamor for jobs...pretty much *any* job so long as it was honest...and Bill "shared the wealth" by getting me hired on too.

Our primary responsibility was to keep the wood-burning stove supplied with fuel, and later we advanced to other chores.

The Lyon household was situated on 125th NE, while Bill's family lived on about 130th NE...something like about five *long* blocks apart on a very steep road. Tough bike riding!

Not over-burdened with enthusiasm, we'd pedal to the bakery and proceed to clean out ovens, pans, counters, and floors as needed, which was just about most of the time.

The pay for our efforts was bags full of day-old bakery goods... part to enjoy on the spot, and the rest to take home to share with our families. A pretty nice contribution to our family's resources for boys of about twelve!

(Sometimes we lucked out and also got the price of a **movie!!**)

Up on the House Top ...
...sooner or later
... it just had to happen ...

Dave Milne

In days of yore, many long years ago, my dear wife Dee and I decided we'd do something special for our friends who were raising small children. Namely, arrange for Santa Claus to drop in on their households just before Christmas for the delight of all.

"Santa Claus" was to be me. I'd get decked out in the traditional red outfit with white fur lining, black boots (ditto with white fur tops), belt, hat, big white (fake) beard and wig, and jolly pillows bulking me up. I'd grip a large canvas bag with jingle bells, stuffed with little wrapped presents, some of which *just happened* to have tags with the children's names, and signed by Santa Claus.

Dee was to be "Mrs. Claus." She was the getaway driver. At the time, we were using a 1967 Ford Bronco with four-wheel drive (essential if there was snow). She was seldom seen, so she didn't need to be wearing her North Pole outfit.

Our very first outing launched us on repeat performances that stretched out over the next 10 years or so. That's when we realized that this was something we were really meant to do in life! We began by surprising some friends who had a young girl age 11 and a boy age 9, completely unexpected by them. The date? The evening of December 23. The time? After dark.

KNOCK... KNOCK.KNOCK
"Huh? Who's that at our door at this time of night?"

Click…Creak.Creak.

"HO! HO! HO! Mr. and Mrs. _____!!! Oh my goodness, I'm surprised to find you all up and still awake! I'm just here to inspect your chimney, for … tomorrow night, you know!" All followed by the most joyously-charmed reaction imaginable, oldsters and youngsters alike, and a "Welcome, Mr. Claus! Come on in!"

From that first moment—and from then on—I knew without knowing how I knew, how Mr. Claus would respond to every question. "How about this chair here, Mr. Claus?"

"HO.HO.HO! Why this is a better chair than my one down at Sears! Thank you!"

Their children were almost speechless. Astonished! Overjoyed! Then … dawning recognition "aww … what's your *real* name?" They kept asking that.

Finally Santa said, "Well, everybody calls me Santa Claus, but … my real name is **Nicholas**."

Very wide eyes! "*Saint* Nicholas?!!" they both asked. Santa nodded.

The rest of the visits that evening were as magical and heart-warming as that one.

Dee and I quickly fell into the routine that Santa and Mrs. Claus themselves must have had for those last few days before Christmas Eve. We always went on December 23. … not the 24th … the night before Christmas … no. That special night was reserved for all families, and their friends and relatives, for their own special traditions. The 23rd was close enough to Christmas, that Santa's chimney inspection seemed reasonable.

After that first year, we always called the parents or guardians in advance and got their permission for Santa's visit. Besides removing any worries that the guy at the door might be a criminal intruder in disguise, these calls were wonderful *seasonal connections* with our friends—and provided critical "advance intel." Such as: "Kathy's friends Beth and Sara will be here for a sleepover!" Or "Billy got a prize in first grade this week!" Or an older child was home from college. Or the wife's mother "Louise is her name"—would be there. Or the neighbors, Don and Cheryl "Don is the guy with a white mustache." Ho-ho-ho Santa always went prepared for all of that!

The weeks before Christmas we were busy elves: purchasing, wrapping, and labeling of little gifts for children and sometimes grandparents. Studying guest lists. Preparing Santa's book—a big leather-bound book cover with an old-looking pad inside. And finally, suiting up for the night's visits.

I can tell you that a strange transformation came over me as that sun on the evening of December 23 was slowly sinking in the west and darkness was creeping over the land. After days of stuffing the sack with gifts and making a list and checking it twice ... I *became* Santa Claus. Not just pretending any more, actually transforming into the real guy!!

Knock…Knock.Knock. Creak. "Oh my gosh it's SANTA CLAUS! Come in, Santa, come in!" She quickly hugged Santa and whispered, "*This is for Myra. We didn't know she'd be here.*" (Then she secretly snuck Santa a small gift.)

"HO HO HO! Well! This *is* a surprise! I thought you'd all be asleep at this hour!"

Ho ho ho! Greetings charmed astonished children flocking around, and for ten minutes or so, all of the warmth and magic of Christmas that a household could possibly have filled the room. Santa would inspect the chimney, "It all seems okay."

"Children would ask, "Are you going to go up it?!!"

"No honey, not tonight. I can't do that tonight."

"Ohhh!" Disappointed heads drooped.

"But tomorrow night I can! Want to know why I can do that tomorrow night?"

Wide eyes bulged above swelling smiles!

"Because tomorrow night ... *I'm magic!*"

"OHHHH!"

"Then, boys and girls, I just happen to have a few gifts for you that I was going to bring tomorrow night. Do you mind if I leave them with you tonight? You can put them under your Christmas tree. They're here in my sack."

Santa always had one for each child who received it with great joy. The bag also had gifts with blank tags for every unexpected child, like this time: "Oh, my goodness! I forgot to write your name on it, Sweetheart. Can you just remind old Santa, and I'll do that?" Santa wrote her name.

There actually was a real Louise...she was the grandmother mentioned earlier. Santa greeted her, "Merry Christmas, Louise! It is so good to see you again. We sure are old friends, aren't we?" No gift for her, just a very warm reunion between her and the *special someone* that she, too, had known as a child many years ago. Here we were again, just before Christmas renewing old acquaintance. She felt so special that Santa recognized her in front of her awed grandchildren. "Wow, Grandma knows Santa from Christmases past!" She was someone exceptionally special that evening.

Santa's departure-ritual was always the same: sack over his shoulder, HoHoHo to the front door, open door, turn, raise one hand and proclaim, "*Merry Christmas to all! And to all a good night!*" Then the exit into the dark night beyond.

The effects on grownups, guests, children, relatives, everyone in the room? Utterly unexpected when Dee and I started this fun of creating memories that lasted for lifetimes! Parents were blown away by the energized, astonished awe of their children. They themselves were caught up in the ...magically transported back to their own childhoods, experiencing magic!

Santa's last stops included a few adult friends. These were usually without advance warning. For these visits, Mr. and Mrs. Claus went together. At the last stop one night, we appeared at the door of two characters who were having a Christmas party! "SANTA! **MRS. CLAUS!** COME IN! COME IN! HO! HO! HO!

The living room overflowed with friends from Evergreen State College and others unknown to us, all of them amazed and thinking their hosts had arranged it! So, for a few warm, welcomed moments of our own, there we were, good cheer and adult merriment abounding. Then merry old St. Nicholas said, "You know, old Santa sometimes gets a little bored with good little boys and girls. Have any of you been *naughty* this year?"

"Oh, yes!!" There was an enthusiastic chorus, predominantly by women!!

"Ho! Ho! Ho! How refreshing! Here's your reward!" (Santa tossed the unclaimed blank-tagged gifts from the sack to the guests.) "Ho! Ho! Ho! Back to the North Pole! Everybody...Merry Christmas to all and to all a good night!"

There were many more magical moments and laughable mishaps during these outings than can be told here. But the one that concludes this story is the one named in the Title. At the end of one of those late December 23rd nights, Santa's rounds completed, and it was time to go home, Dee asked if I'd like to get out of the Santa suit for the ride home. For some reason, I said "No! How often do you get to be Santa Claus? I'll just enjoy it for a few more minutes." And we headed home.

About eight inches of snow covered the ground. Our home at the time was an isolated, rustic cabin on the shore of Oyster Bay, WA. We arrived, put the Bronco in the carport, and tramped through the deep snow down a couple of short stairways to the house.

"OH, NO. We're locked out!"

We knew that an upstairs bedroom window was unlocked. To reach it, one had to go over the roof of the main cabin. We got a ladder from the carport, and Up On the House Top I went. So, there was Santa Claus…on top of a snow-covered roof, under a cold, silent, night-sky sparkling with stars…right by the chimney, surrounded by tall, snow-covered firs, pausing for just a moment to belt out: **Ho! Ho! Ho!**

All was well.

Let It Go

Verl Rogers

In a doctor's waiting room, I sat next to a lady working on a jigsaw puzzle. She looked not my type, but I opened a conversation anyway. I said, "That puzzle looks impossible. All the pieces look the same color and the same shape.

She replied, "Oh no. If you look closely, you can find little differences. Already I have put in five pieces." She changed the subject. "Isn't it a fine day?"

"Well, yes," was my response. "I sat out on a bench in the sun and took a nap. You can, too. The day is perfect just to sit in the sun. We don't often have sunlight like this in November."

A pleasant conversation followed, and I decided the lady was less ugly the longer we talked. She told me how pleasant their back porch was on a sunny day.

Then she began about her husband, and went on and on. "He's not beautiful, but he behaves that way. He's always gentle, doesn't swear, goes to school events with me. He was PTA president a couple of years. I have been lucky ever since we started dating in college."

The lady told me that she went through a bad time recently where she had a cancer and then chemotherapy in the local oncology clinic. "The cancer has gone, but I was sure sour for a while. I kept thinking how much better I was in my twenties and thirties. I was forty, and in my eyes, I was a has-been. I hovered and got stuck on pain, woe and misery. One day my husband yelled at me, 'Quit it! You've got me and the kids, and I have a good job, and the house is nearly paid for, and why are you still so gloomy? Just cheer up!'"

The light dawned on me as she talked. I was fretting about the same losses, pain, sickness. Why? What did I gain from thinking about poor me? Let go of those ideas that I am miserable! Just let go!

Verl Rogers. November 9, 2016. Permission to reprint.

Ernest "Ernie" Becker #1

Jeanne D. Thompson

My father, Ernie Becker, was a long-time architect, builder, photographer, good parent, good friend, honest to the core and the nicest guy you'd ever want to meet.

His young life was lived during a hard time. His father deserted his mother and three siblings during the depression and Ernie had to go to work to support them. He managed to graduate high school. When he was fourteen, he and his brother rode bicycles from Michigan to Missouri to visit their father and it was the last time Ernie was to see him.

During and after high school, he worked as a telegraph messenger and eventually met and married my mother. He lost my mother in childbirth and grieved for months and truly, his whole life. During the war he designed airplanes and specifically a fuel system that wouldn't freeze. The US sent many planes to Alaska where they were parked until needed. My father's fuel system worked and his company's planes were the only ones to leave the ground. Later, he traveled the world designing shipping ports, rivers, dams, and public buildings, in addition to residences in California.

While at Panorama Retirement, he was a busy and popular fellow. He served as the Chinook Building Resident Council representative, <u>designed</u> a beautiful bench for our old Convalescent and Rehabilitation Center and a narthex table for resident Don Stern to build for the Lacey Community Church. He was an avid wood worker. He constructed the wardrobe rooms behind the Panorama Quinault

Building Auditorium stage. He had many, many friends.

My dad had a 'good death'. The staff at the Panorama C&R gave him superb care. I sat with him for four days and was with him when he died. The nursing staff made sure he was without pain, warm and comfortable. On Wednesday, he became alert and oriented. I sat on the floor next to him and we had a very nice chat about all kinds of things; politics (we always talked politics), COVID 19 (which he hadn't heard about), family status (about all the children and grandchildren) and extended family. I told him I'd found his father, finally. He was pleased to know his father died in 1965 in Quincy, IL. Dad took a nap that afternoon and never woke up again. He slept. He breathed until he stopped.

I am missing him.

Addition to "Ernie" Memory #2

Jeanne D. Thompson

My father, Ernest Lawrence Becker, was born September 9, 1917, at Sibley Memorial Hospital, Washington, DC.

His young life was *lived*. He managed to graduate from Godwin Heights High School in Grand Rapids, MI, in 1935. He learned to type in high school. He was the only boy in typing class. He also learned to set type for printing presses prior to the invention of Linotype.

My paternal *grandfather* changed his name to "Lee" Becker. He built a house trailer and became a traveling house-to-house salesman of his own boxes of laundry soap, among other things. He had a small printing press in the back of the trailer and *printed his own soap boxes!*

In the spring of 1933, my *father* Ernest (at 16) and his younger brother, Mervin, with $5.00 from their mother, joined his father and his father's girlfriend. They traveled Illinois, Indiana and Wisconsin that summer. My father, Ernest, set the type and printed the small two-inch boxes, which were filled from *large* "Super Suds" boxes purchased from a grocery store for 79 cents. They sold their small boxes of "Super Cleaner" for 25 cents, house to house.

Occasionally they printed flyers for local merchants. "Anything to make a buck in the 30's!" They could eat at White Castle for $0.05 coffee, $0.10 pie, and $0.15 hamburger. They could all eat out for twenty-five to thirty-five cents each at White Castle and many other places.

In late August of that year, they were in Madison, WI, and it was time for the boys to go to school. They left Madison on their bicycles and prepared to head for Grand Rapids, MI, through Chicago, IL. Grandfather Lee started them out for about 35 miles driving his car with ropes hooked to the door handle with Ernest holding on to another *release rope.*

Grandfather Lee thought the boys would encounter wild dogs, so he helped them fill water pistols with water and ammonia. They didn't see wild dogs, but they did see a mean pack of *six boys* in Chicago who wanted their bikes. They used their water pistols on them and got away. They had tried not to hit the pack's eyes!

In those days there were no freeways, just roads and highways, mostly unpaved! There were very few automobiles. Most drivers who helped the boys had them ride *in* the car or truck with their bicycles *tied* onto the vehicle. They subsisted often on the generosity of farmers who allowed them to sleep in the barn—"If they had no matches." This usually included dinner and breakfast!

Once, in applying for a place to stay at a local police station, they slept on a courtroom bench.

The rest of the trip was uneventful, and they arrived in Grand Rapids with their mother's $5 intact—in time to enroll in school!

Christmas on the Ranch

Lucy Reuter

It was 1943 and America was in the throes of World War II. My dad and uncle were serving overseas, and my mother, sister Susie and I were temporarily camping out with my aunt and two cousins in their small house in El Paso, Texas.

It would soon be Christmas. Mom and Aunt Neppy had decided that we would spend it on our grandparents' ranch in New Mexico. We cousins were not so sure we liked the idea. We'd have to leave our friends and warm El Paso to go spend Christmas on an isolated ranch in cold New Mexico. Besides, Nannie and Tom had no electricity and everything was powered with propane gas. How could we have a tree with no lights? What if the pump to the well gave out and we had to use the outhouse! UGH!

The adults won out and off we went to the ranch. Four kids, ages 13, 14, and two 10-year-olds, two adults, the presents, and Christmas decorations were crammed into Mom's Oldsmobile. Talk about sardines!

We finally arrived, after a four-hour trip, to delicious smells coming from the kitchen. Nannie was a great cook!

The first day, we piled into the back of the pickup truck (no seat belts in those days), and drove across the pasture to cut down the tree. Once we got it trimmed, with all the hoarded tinsel and decorations, it was a sight to behold!

Nonnie and Tom had a party and invited all the neighboring ranchers. They came with gusto, each bringing something good to eat. We bundled up and rode the horses. We helped corral the sheep. We played marathon games of monopoly and rummy, and ate goodies to our hearts' content. Combining three sugar rations helped out in that department. Much to our surprise we had a wonderful time, and the pump held out.

And then it struck! The blizzard to beat all blizzards! The ranch was eight miles from the highway on a narrow dirt road, which was now covered with ice and snow. How would we get home? We had stayed a week. My grandmother's pantry would hold out for her and Tom, but certainly not another week for our hungry bunch.

But my wonderful grandfather had seen bigger predicaments than this in his 70 years. He hitched up the team of horses to our car and away we went over that snow-packed road to the highway.

We arrived home to spend New Year's Eve in warm El Paso, in time for us kids to ruin all Aunt Neppy's pots and pans ringing in the New Year. But that is another story.!

My Romance

Verl Rogers

The song "My Romance" from a Broadway play struck me when I was young.

"My romance doesn't need to have a moon in the sky...

My romance doesn't need a thing but you!"

That romance and those words came true for me when I was 26 and fell in love with Janet Bixler.

"Oh, Verl, I think I love you!" she said, and I said the same to her. After a day of deep thinking, I asked her to marry me and she said "Yes, yes."

Our engagement lasted until the September wedding, and we managed to hold our embraces to kissing. We held to the old rule, No Sleeping Together until the Wedding!

Such restraint was old-fashioned even in the 1950's. I recall one morning at sunup that summer. We had slept in the Bixler home, she in her old bedroom and me on a couch in the sewing room. We met in the hall, in pajamas, embraced and kissed. I was happy to find her in clingy garments, but that was as far as we went.

Looking back from age 93, I believe the old rule has merit.

We had a church wedding, both families present and a church full of friends. The priest used a wedding rite from an old prayer book, where we said, "...'til death do us part, and thereto I pledge thee my troth."

A few years later I recall, Janet and I had a big fight, but when we were both hot Janet said, "Let's look at our wedding vows." We did, and found "...'til death do us part." That settled us, immediately. We never had such a hot argument again.

We lived together for 58 years until she died. You can call it marital bliss. Certainly, it was romance. It may have been at our fortieth year that we said, "Let's grow old together." We did grow old together, and I enjoyed the time. Though I know of two or three couples married over fifty years, they seem rare. Janet and I were lucky.

Janet died of a virus pneumonia in 2012. My memories are mostly happy; seldom do I recall the bad times.

Verl Rogers. August 14, 2020. Permission to print.

Tantan's Teasers and Treasures

Mary Jo Shaw

One of the most influential people in my life was my aunt Mary Ann Kathryn (Tantan) Osborn. She was born October 24, 1913, in San Antonio, TX. To her I owe my deep love of piano which I taught for 55 years and continue to play for others. She was a major inspiration for my treasured 13 years as a Sister of Divine Providence. You will enjoy a few of my pleasant memories and her *wholesale, unplanned* teasers and treasures:

The first day of her move to Our Lady of the Lake Convent nursing home in San Antonio, TX:

The cherished approximately 36" x 30" painting that had hung over the fireplace in the Osborn Family home on Ripley Ave in San Antonio, was hung over her bed in the Sisters' nursing home. The first day she entered the room, her mouth opened with joy, when my cousin Ann Osborn VanDelist, (who had prepared her room) walked Tantan inside.

"There He is!" Tantan exclaimed. Her arms opened wide, as were the arms of the Sacred Heart of Jesus in the large vintage oil painting. She was satisfied, calm, and *at home* with the reminder that He was there, too.

Sister Clair, (Tantan and Mom's sister) was retired in the same building. What a blessed day for all of us, knowing she could be living her last days with love, protection, care, chapel, activities, and we'd be able to visit her often.

Tantan was in the nursing home with the Sisters of Divine Providence:

She and I were strolling down the hall. She noticed the sign on the supply-room door and read aloud, "This door must be kept locked at all times."

She looked up at me with furrowed brow...and an imp in her eyes...and asked, "Then what use it? Why don't they get rid of it?"

———

We sat enjoying pages of my family photos together in the Sisters' day room:

Tantan pointed to the photo of my sister Peggy on the far left...only half of Peggy's face was showing in the photo. Tantan grinned and side-smiled remarking, "That's just a *sample* of Peggy!"

———

In the Sisters' exercise room, the therapist asked Tantan, "Can you count to 10 with me while we do exercises?" The impish smile appeared again, "Can you do the Irish Jig?' Outside we sat reminiscing in the shade of the large pecan trees on a swirling windy day. "Look at those bushes wrestling with each other!" She didn't have to dig deep to unearth an appropriate creative comment. I still cherish her teasing remarks, and wish I had written them down all of those years.

———

"Everyone here is so capable, and they use it!" expressed her kind feelings of living her last years with the Sisters. She went to her long-awaited new home in heaven on April 30, 2003, at age 89.

P.S. In a higher branch of my family tree, my Aunt Maggie Scanlon was born in Ireland **on St. Patrick's Day!** At my grandparent's home, Tantan thumped the Irish Jig on her hefty Griffin upright piano, while enthusiastic shoes thinned the rug on their living room floor. Sounds of Irish songs and O Danny Boy filled the room. We young ones wore green crepe-paper skirts and streamers. Even the men and women donned anything green from hats to bracelets, ties, bows...down to the socks. We can only smile at black and white photos, but the emeralds are still painted in our photographic minds. Those were the days!

Four Favorite Shorties

Candy Berner

When I was a young child, my mother frequently made oven-broiled toasted cheese sandwiches using Velveeta cheese, of course. On one of those occasions, we didn't realize a mouse had gotten into our oven. He was broiled right along with the cheese sandwiches. What a smell! To this day I cannot eat a toasted cheese sandwich because I remember that awful cooked-mouse smell. I think of this incident every time I hear the words "toasted cheese sandwich" and laugh to myself.

———

Can't believe my mother actually did this, but she told the story to us many times:

As a young bride, my mother moved from the East Coast to Port Orchard, Washington, to wait for my dad's ship to dock at the Bremerton Naval Shipyard near the end of WWII. Noticing pretty yellow flowers growing close to the house, she picked a bouquet to set in a jar on the table. After she met my dad and they returned to the house, he noticed the flowers immediately and that the house stunk. Mother had never seen skunk cabbage before.

———

I had been hiking all day and had not seen another person. Then Nature called, so I squatted down behind a small bush next to the trail. That is when two people on bicycles came zooming around the corner. I was caught with my britches down. All I could do was smile and wave.

From my youngest years, my sister and I were taught the standard rules of etiquette and general good manners, just in case we were ever invited to a meal at a friend's house. Not everything I might need to know had been covered, though. In first grade, I had dinner at my boyfriend Billy's house. I remember his family asked him to say "grace." Then they asked me if I wanted to say "grace." I had never heard the word before and was confused, so I just said the word "grace."

I don't remember that they laughed at me, though they certainly must have felt like it. When I returned home, I asked my mother what "grace" was all about. Soon after, our family began the practice of saying "grace" before our dinner meal.

Extra Day in My Life

Mary Jo Shaw

This email was to my friend Patricia on Jan. 2, 2015. In the letter, Verl is the 87-year-old man I sponsored in 2014 to become a Catholic. We live at Panorama Seniors and have not had a car since 2012.

Hi, Patricia!

You asked how my day was. You won't believe. I got up early at 7 this morning to wash my hair, put on a nice pull-over sweater for church tonight and had to leave the message to remind Verl to pick me up for church. He called back <u>late</u> this afternoon and insisted it was Friday, not Saturday. I began to feel sorry for him—he must be losing it. I looked at my calendar, and it said Friday. Poor Verl!

I started to call my neighbor Elaine to ask to go with her tomorrow for *Sunday* Mass. But then I began to ask myself whether **I** was wrong. I rechecked the calendar. Yes, it said *Friday*. But how did I know I was looking at the right square? I had my DO-LIST with *Saturday* written at the top.

AHA! My computer would tell me.

I melted. **I** had lost it and needed to go find myself. But where do I go?—and should I go Friday or Saturday? I still can't believe that yesterday was New Year's Day. Verl was right. It *is* Friday.

Then it dawned on me. GREAT!! I CAN USE AN EXTRA DAY IN MY LIFE—WHY FIGHT IT?!?

I practiced piano to prepare to record another DVD for Panorama TV next week. Then plopped into my recliner by my patio door with my laptop. I had that *extra day* to work on my book memoir Convent to Catwalk.

I glanced outside—it was dark.

You asked how my day was. Go figure. Let me know whether it was a good one. Gaining an extra day is always good. I discovered it for myself, and hope I get another one...SOON!

My new year has started out great. Have a good day!

Mary Jo, Friday, I hope, Jan. 2, 2015

Life's Greatest Embarrassment

Candy Berner

One sunny summer Saturday afternoon our family of four drove to Tacoma to visit an open house on a naval ship that had pulled into dock and was giving tours. My dad had been a sailor and thought his two daughters would like to see a huge ship up close. What my sis and I noticed were the sailors. I was thirteen and my sis a year younger. As we walked along the sidewalk, two sailors in their dress whites passed by us. As I turned my head to feast my eyes upon these handsome creatures, I didn't notice the large garbage can on the sidewalk directly in my path which made a racket when I rammed into it. Luckily the trash can didn't fall over and spill its contents and the only casualty was my great embarrassment!

Mama and the Blue Mercury

Lucy Reuter

My mother, Lucy Judson, was the daughter of an indomitable woman. She was the daughter of a West Texas rancher and was also an Army wife, a combination which gave her determination and spunk. She enjoyed new experiences and rarely took no for an answer. At the age of 12 she had learned to drive, and from then on had a love for automobiles.

When we arrived in Germany in 1947 to join my father, she was determined that we would travel and soak up as much of the culture as we could. The only problem was that our 1940 Oldsmobile was "ailing" and did not take well to the PX gasoline. This left us with a dilemma, as the trains were not very reliable in those days. However, unbeknownst to Mom, this problem was about to be solved.

The Army Headquarters in Frankfurt sent a message to all the military casernes that a large shipment of Fords was being delivered to an automobiles dealer in Amsterdam, and a certain number was being allotted for Americans to purchase. Dad immediately submitted our name for the lottery. I think Mom must have spent a lot of time on her knees, because we were one of the lucky families to have our name drawn. All the future car owners gathered in Frankfurt and took the train to Amsterdam. Mother was not very thrilled with the idea of driving a stripped-down Ford, instead of her well-loved Oldsmobile, but she knew this was the solution to our transportation needs.

When they arrived at their destination, they were ushered into the car lot and were met with a sea of black Fords. Sitting in the midst of them was a beautiful royal blue Mercury. Mother took one look at the Mercury and decided that was the car for her.

The language barrier was no deterrent. She approached the car dealer and pointed to the Mercury, and he pointed to himself, meaning it was his car. She took out her wallet, implying that she was willing to pay him more money. He nodded his head. Mother stepped into the restroom, removed her emergency cash from her "bosom buddy," and became the proud owner of the blue Mercury. That car provided us with reliable transportation for our two years in Europe, and she was able to take my sister and me on trips to France, Austria, Switzerland, and Italy. When we left Germany, the Mercury became the property of another lucky owner.

Upon our arrival in the United States, our family reverted to their allegiance to General Motors, but Mom never forgot the blue Mercury and delighted in telling the story of how she had acquired it.

Music for the Ages

Mary Jo Shaw

Lunch was over. Normally, the dining room in Assisted Living was cleared, but most residents sat listening.

Tears in my eyes welled up. *Lord, playing piano is such a simple thing. You've given me the talent and the joy of sharing it. Each note I play is for Your honor and glory.*

A typical day is a shot in the arm that keeps me returning:

As I entered the lunch room, a gentleman leaned toward his wife's good ear, "The piano lady's here today—we're going to have good music." She turned. I threw a hearty wave.

Woman in blue grabbed my arm, "I want to take this time before you start to thank you for coming. I enjoy everything you play. I always get here early on Mondays."

Purple-hat-lady sat tall, beaming from ear to ear, and gestured a welcome with both closed fists from across the room.

The melodies softly floated and mingled with the warm smells of roasting menu foods emanating from the nearby small kitchen. I caught a remark from the men's table-for-four, while I played a challenging section of *The Impossible Dream*. In a pleasant tone, one slowly said to another, *"The older I get, the more that song touches my heart. My wife and I danced to it at our wedding...and..."* I had to focus on my music and block out listening to the rest of his conversation. The round of applause from that table spoke louder than the words I had missed.

A former singer and his wife always sat close by. Once, they showed up ten minutes late. Disappointed, he pulled out her chair, "Oh, we missed the first numbers." She was already humming along *As Time Goes By*, alternating soft, whistling tones like a bird.

I play full arrangements of old time popular, favorites, musicals, hymns, some jazz and rags that I know they enjoy. After I finished Chopin's slow, four-page, *Nocturne in E-Flat*, a recently-new resident lady at the second table whispered as she finished eating and passed by the piano, "I'm not a classics lover, but I must admit that's my favorite today. I enjoy any numbers you play."

"Mine, too," her friend emphatically nodded.

In Gentle Care (the Alzheimer/Dementia) unit, I'm touched at the response from several delicate residents who don't always seem receptive, despite their loving care. Then I see a foot start tapping, or a head lean back with a big smile and closed eyes. Or I hear little Ms. B humming clear as a lark from her wheeled chair with her dancing eyes on me and her hand on my electronic piano. I know she's someone's mother, sister, aunt. She could be my mother—and my music is making her happy.

As I headed down the hall after playing, I was called back. The same Ms. B grabbed my arm with watery, red eyes, "Please don't go. We're not finished yet." I looked into her eyes, "I promise, I'll come back and play again." She gave me a beautiful, false-teeth-showing smile.

The *first* time I played in our Convalescent and Rehabilitation Center, I began playing that long, Chopin *Nocturne*. Immediately, Joe wheeled himself just two feet from the electronic piano. He stared me down the entire length of the composition.

Other residents were still, with pleasant, soft smiles in their wheeled chairs around the white-clothed tables topped with little plates of Oreos. So motionless, I wondered if they were still breathing.

After the last soft measures faded away, the entire room exploded with a huge resounding applause. They were far from sleeping and certainly *were* breathing! Joe brought his chair even closer and begged loudly, "Play that one again."

I smiled, "If they let me come back, I promise—I'll play it again."

And I always do.

Playing music gives me far more joy than I know it gives to my aged family of friends.

I'm simply sharing the talent God has given me. Born in 1939, I thank Him every day, many times, and I never want to take it for granted.

Truly, I am blessed.

Emily's Salad and Shoes

Emily Shaw, age 14

Hmmm, Granny Jo, I don't remember a specific time when this happened, but it reminded me of when you and Pawpaw were at our house once, and we were having salad. But there wasn't any dressing on it. So, Pawpaw went to go get some, and came back with some balsamic vinaigrette. It was in those salad dressing bottles that just have a huge hole in it once you open the cap. But Pawpaw didn't know that. He went to pour what he thought was a little dressing. Instead, he poured about 1/3 of a plate full of dressing!

Love you so much, Granny Jo!!!
Emily

———

Hi, Granny!

I just remembered another funny story entry last night, when we were talking about what we did in our childhood. What I remembered was this: One time when you came over to our house, you taught me how to tie my shoes. This new, wonderful discovery led to my tying everyone's shoes that I could find. Mommy was going on a walk, and to show off that I could tie shoes, I asked if I could tie hers for her. Mommy obligingly said I could, and after I tied both of them, she stood up, winced, and said they were a little too tight. (I like shoes to be tied super tight.) I said that I could fix them, and so I did. Mommy went on her walk with her shoes, probably not very neatly tied. To this day, whenever I think of tying my shoes, I still think of that funny occurrence.

Love you lots!!!
Emily

Copacabana and Extras!

Evelyn Peterson

Evelyn Peterson is a first cousin to my husband, Chris Shaw. The three of us look forward to phone calls about every two weeks. Evelyn is legally blind at 93, living with her daughter Faye Lynn and granddaughter Leigh in Kentucky. During Covid 19, I interviewed her for this book.

Evelyn, you're so sharp with an alert memory. Besides your story of travel-encounters where you sat in over a dozen unusual, unique "seats," you also experienced happenings most of us never imagined. Tell me about some of them.

She began at random, selecting November 1948, giving us a nutshell explanation of New York nightclubs, pinpointing the Copacabana, and her matchless, rare experiences:

I was one of the Chorus Girls who danced at the Copacabana. New Yorkers called us *Copa Bunnies!* We were the main performers, and three of the *five* numbers each night, and had "in-between, fillers":

1. Chorus Girls—our 1st performance. We always opened the show in beautiful costumes and headpieces—I'll explain a little later.

2. In-between-act/filler (which gave us a chance to rest) provided great, excellent variety, such as professional magicians, singers, or other dancers.

3. Chorus Girls—our 2nd performance and different dance steps.

4. Headline comedians act—Dean Martin and Jerry Lewis! When

their contracted time expired, the famous singer Lena Horne performed.

5. Chorus Girls—our 3rd performance, again different dance steps. We were the night's Finale.

Oh, Mary Jo, I remember as if it were yesterday. One night the magician had left a card on the floor. When I did my very high kick, I slipped on that card, and both feet went up. I plopped down on my butt. Of course, we were professionals and knew to pop up and keep going again.

After I retrieved my position dancing, I kept hearing people in the small audience whispering something like, "sshe...ssshee, sshe.." Soon, I realized the hook and eye at the top of the zipper on my Carmen Miranda long, heavy, full skirt had broken. I could feel the zipper slowly *opening* from the top to bottom.

Every time we danced, it took *both* hands to hold our headpieces: a basket of paper mache fruits...bananas, apples, oranges, and pineapples. Now still executing an energetic, fast dance, I had to maneuver with only one hand holding the basket of fruits, and the other hand trying to hold together the back of my heavy skirt. And actually, I DID...keeping in step.

We all had a position in the line-up. Looking from the audience, I was in the front row, left corner of the dance floor.

Evelyn, what skill and talent! And what a story. But what's the difference between a Chorus Girl and a Show Girl?

Show Girls wear skimpy costumes, and are in other night clubs, not in the Copacabana.

Oh, Show Girls *show* more skin?

Well, yes. And Chorus Girls have three requirements:

    Kick high.

    Wear false eye lashes.

    Be 5' 6" tall and thin.

But, Evelyn, you aren't that tall. How did you get to be one of the dancers?

I'm only 5' 3". You know from modeling yourself how an agent sends you to interviews for modeling shows, commercials, TV work, photo pictures for ads, billboards, and so forth. Sometimes we had "open calls" when anyone at all can go for an interview.

Oh, yes! We called them *cattle calls*! We got a numbered ticket. We didn't like those and I only went to one or two. Too many hours to wait all of the time.

Well, I went to one and got chosen because of my really high kick, dance ability, false eyelashes and had a portfolio of photos and a long list of experiences.

Did you have any other mishaps?

Oh yes, embarrassing at the time, but fun to tell now. Saturday nights were always quite crowded at the Copacabana. Remember that our floor shared space with the patrons' tables, thus less space for us dancers. Our colorful Carmen Miranda skirts were trimmed with a lace-like, eyelet embroidery with open holes. Our tops were bra-like of the same bright colors. When I swung around, that eyelet trim on the bottom of my skirt caught onto a lady's beaded dress. Beads flung like a swarm of bees. Imagine dancing on a floor full of beads!

We did wear light weight, flowing chiffon costumes for our romantic, slower dances.

I remember on another Saturday's full-house...my Carmen Miranda skirt swept a customer's steak—right onto the dance floor! I forgot the owner's name, but my good friend told me he said, "There goes Evelyn again. But she's so good, pretty, has big smiles, and everybody loves her."

Evelyn, that's hilarious! Weren't you featured in a magazine at one time?

Oh, yes! One evening, LIFE magazine writers attended our entire show at Copacabana to do a story on Dean Martin and Jerry Lewis. But they decided to do a story on me, instead. I told them, "But I'm going back to Texas!" Was I ever lucky! They still interviewed me and took several photos. About five months later the magazine came out with President Truman on the cover...and my story and pictures were on the inside!

What an honor as the top Chorus Girl at Copacabana, New York! What about the movies and the NEWSREELS?

In the 40's and 50's there were no TV's, to see the news. We just had radios. You remember going to the movies. Between the showings, we watched the NEWSREEL. It was always week-old news. But for about 15 minutes, we could actually *see* the battlefields, the horse races, sporting events, world series, beauty contests, countries around the world, Macy's and California's parades!"

I'd go to the movies to see myself in the NEWSREEL winning the beauty contests, or they'd have a segment called This Is America. These were actually advertising for businesses in New York. For instance, I was pretending to visit various fortune tellers in New York. Another time, I was dressed elegantly holding an Irish Setter at the Westchester Country Club in New York.

The NEWSREEL also showed Tony Pasteur's musical with us dressed in beautiful Arab costumes...but in black and white, of course.

These were local (New York) settings, since TV networks had not spread around the nation yet.

You told me years ago about other contests and events. Refresh us on some of those.

Let me think. Well, among 52 contestants I won the title of Miss Modern Venus 1946 at Steeplechase Park, Coney Island. I won $200. At 19 years old in 1946, I felt I'd won a million dollars!

TV was so new, probably winning that contest, lead my agent to book me for the publicized production of NBC's "Last Man on Earth." Only the one man, animals and birds were left, and kids were needed to play the animals. I was a bat.

Then I got onto TV's Campus Hoopla in New York on Friday nights. The setting was a soda counter with teens singing and dancing. That lasted a year and a half.

There was a time when TV had no sponsors. US KEDS shoes was the first pay-for-live-ads shown. Eventually, we held up sandwich boards while someone read them aloud for other live commercials.

Burt Parks sat behind a desk on his show to interview several of us sitting, also. The lights were extremely bright. Thus, we wore "pancake," dark, face-makeup, because we *faded* in those lights. My face was so close to those lights, the glue on one of my false eyelashes melted and dangled in front of my eye. I quickly tore it off, jerked my head backward, and snatched off the other eyelash.

Oh, Evelyn, I could write a book on your life.

We both came back to reality with laughter and memories.

"I love you, Evelyn. What a fun day ahead writing up these great stories. God bless you."

"Mary Jo, I had such a good time. You made my day. I love you, and God bless you, too."

NOTE:

It will take a few seconds to Google:

Life Magazine. November 1948. Evelyn Peterson.

See headline, sharp pictures, and read Evelyn's story.

Chita Knew

Lucy Reuter

It was 1947, and my mother, sister and I were on our way to Germany to join my father, who was stationed there with the U. S. Army Occupation Forces. We were very excited, but also sad…one member of our family could not go. In those days military families were not allowed to ship their pets overseas.

Through the grapevine, my mother found a family willing to give a home to our Boston Bull Terrier, Chita. We made our sad farewells and set off on our journey. We enjoyed our two and a half years there, but often thought of Chita and how much we missed her.

Fast forward to October 1949; it was time to return to the good old U.S of A. We would be visiting my grandparents in El Paso, Texas before moving on to Ft. Knox, Kentucky, where my dad had been assigned. El Paso was still a small town in those days, and when relatives came to visit, their family would often put a short blurb in the newspaper's society page. By chance, Chita's adopted family read about our return and contacted my grandmother. The lady told Grandmother that Chita had been a good pet, but had never really accepted them as her family. She offered to give her back to us if we wanted her!

Upon arrival in El Paso we were ecstatic to learn the news. Mother and I drove over to get Chita. We parked in front of the house. I opened the car door, turned to Mom and asked, "Do you think Chita will remember us?" At that moment, Chita came flying across their back-yard fence and into the car. She snuggled under my mother's feet and would not budge.

Chita was home!

From that day forward, when a suitcase appeared by the door, Chita attached herself to it and refused to move. She was not going to be left behind again.

Chita died at the ripe old age of fourteen and a half…our faithful companion to the end.

Heart's Desire

Lois Williams

"One thing have I desired of the LORD, that will I seek after; that I may dwell in the house of the LORD all the days of my life, to behold the beauty of the LORD, and to enquire in His temple." Psalm 27:4

Small arms wrapped around my neck,
snuggling into my lap, she announced,
"Grandma, I'm finally here.
I can hug you all I want,
and that's all I came for."

Though swelled with joy,
my heart nearly broke,
for deep in my soul
I saw my approach to my Heavenly Father.
His joy when I come to Him
surely is quelled when I simply
haul out my shopping list.
Does He ever hear from me
those tender words?

Father, teach me to snuggle into Your lap
And whisper, "Here I am.
Let me hug You.
My heart's desire

is to feel Your nearness...
and that's all I came for."

Reprinted by permission, from "Psalms From The Pathway",
Xulon Press © 2003 by Lois Williams
Email: fredlowill@msn.com

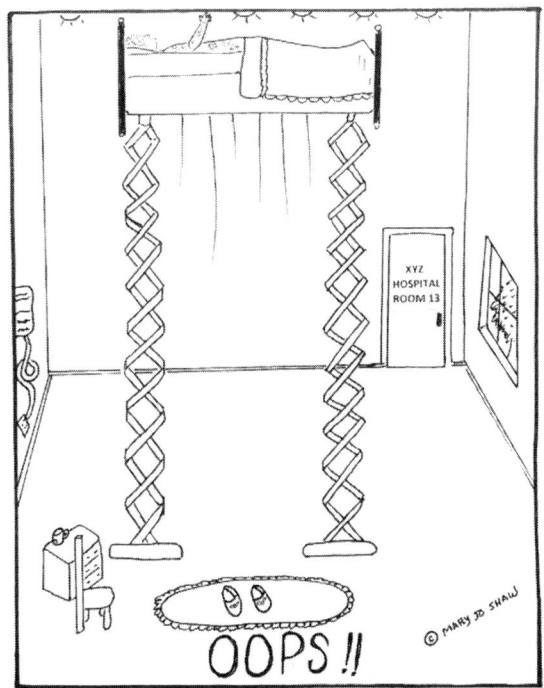

Hospital Bed Drawing "OOPS!" Mary Jo Shaw

This was an actual happening! I was in a hospital room that looked exactly like my drawing. The bed started moving slo-o-o-w-ly up toward the high ceiling. It picked up speed!

Up.........up.....up...up.up.up...

I kept hearing, screech.......screech....screech...screech.screech.

Then my arm reached out and turned off my alarm: in my own bedroom on 5th floor Quinault, Panorama Retirement in 2020!!

(It "actually happened"...in my *dream*.)

DID YOU ENJOY GOOFIES AND GOODIES?

*My best friend is a person who will give me
a BOOK I have not read.*

—Abraham Lincoln

Good, clean *family* books are great for all ages
—men, women, and teens—
for birthdays, Christmas, thank-you, and anytime.

***Goofies and Goodies,
Crossroads to Convent,*** and ***Convent to Catwalk***
are ideal for book clubs, church groups,
the bedridden, the hospitalized, and for those
who love or don't love to read!

How can I help you with my free, fun, book reads/signings,
and/or with easy at-your-event fundraising,
at luncheons, bazaars, schools,
or with bulk orders or purchasing?

Book rates make shipping easy to send anywhere.

Contact me, the author, directly:
Maryjoshaw3@gmail.com